insight text guide

Robert Beardwood & Anica Boulanger-Mashberg

Twelfth Night

William Shakespeare

First published in 2024, reprinted in 2025.

Insight Publications Pty Ltd
3/350 Charman Road
Cheltenham VIC 3192
Australia
Tel: +61 3 8571 4950
Email: books@insightpublications.com.au

www.insightpublications.com.au

William Shakespeare's *Twelfth Night* / Robert Beardwood & Anica Boulanger-Mashberg

Robert Beardwood & Anica Boulanger-Mashberg assert the moral right to be identified as the authors of this work.

ISBNs:
9781923154810 (print)
9781923154803 (digital)

Cover design by Melisa Paredes
Layout by Bec Yule @ Red Chilli Design
Edited by Julia Carlomagno
Proofread by Janice Bird

Proudly printed in Australia by Ligare Book Printers

Insight Publications acknowledges the Traditional Custodians of the Country on which we meet and work, the Boonwurrung People of the Kulin Nation. We pay our respects to their Elders past and present, and extend that respect to all Aboriginal and Torres Strait Islander peoples.

contents

CHARACTER MAP

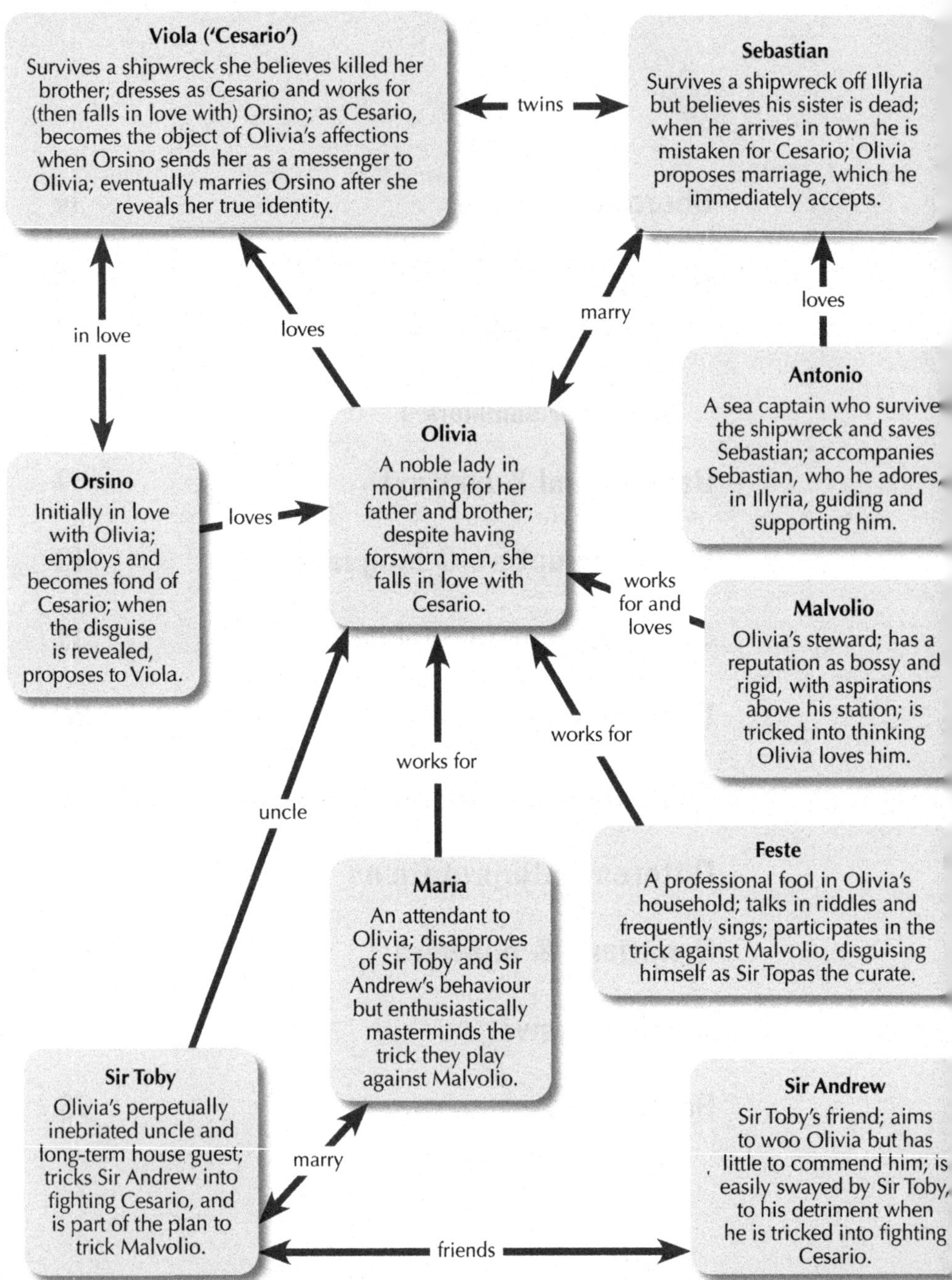

OVERVIEW

About the author

William Shakespeare was an English playwright and actor in the late 1600s and early 1700s. He was born in Stratford-upon-Avon, a town in the English midlands, in 1564. His formal schooling ended in his teens, and he did not go to university. By the 1590s, though, when Shakespeare was around thirty, he was an established playwright and actor in London. Famous plays such as *Romeo and Juliet* and *A Midsummer Night's Dream* were written at this time; the sources they draw on include classical Greek and Roman texts (such as Ovid's *Metamorphoses*), suggesting that Shakespeare had been reading widely.

As well as writing plays, Shakespeare was acting in them and a part-owner of the theatre company known as the Lord Chamberlain's Men (later the King's Men, when Queen Elizabeth I died in 1603). They continued to perform the plays he wrote, including *Hamlet* and *Macbeth*, in the early 1600s. *Twelfth Night* is also thought to have been written at this time, possibly shortly before the death of the Queen.

Shakespeare married Anne Hathaway when he was eighteen and she was twenty-six. Their three children were Susanna and twins Judith and Hamnet. Hamnet died at the age of eleven. Shakespeare's own twins may have been a factor behind the presence of twins in his plays: in addition to Viola and Sebastian in *Twelfth Night*, there are two sets of twins in *The Comedy of Errors*.

Although Shakespeare spent most of his time in London, he retained a strong connection with Stratford. He bought a large house there, known as New Place, in 1596, and during the early 1600s invested in farmland nearby. After his last play, *The Tempest* (first performed in 1611), he spent more time in Stratford. He died after a brief illness – apparently brought about by celebrations at the wedding of his daughter Judith – in 1616.

Only half of Shakespeare's plays were published during his lifetime, in editions known as 'quartos' (a term referencing the book page size) that were based on prompt copies (production copies, containing all the technical cues for a performance) or an actor's – not necessarily reliable – recollection of the dialogue. In 1623, two of Shakespeare's fellow actors published a collection of thirty-six plays known as the First Folio. *Twelfth Night* is one of the plays first published in the First Folio, under its full title: *Twelfth Night, or What You Will*.

A note on the text: quotes and line references throughout this guide refer to the New Cambridge Shakespeare edition of *Twelfth Night* (3rd edn, 2017).

Synopsis

In Illyria, Duke Orsino is enjoying music that makes him think of the woman he loves, Olivia – but she, unfortunately, does not love him. Moreover, mourning her brother, she has sworn to remain veiled and secluded for seven years.

At the same time, Viola arrives on the shores of Illyria, having survived a shipwreck in which she fears her brother drowned. The Captain accompanying her tells her about Orsino and Olivia, and Viola decides to disguise herself as Cesario, a young man, and seek employment at Orsino's court.

At Olivia's house, her relative Sir Toby Belch and her maid, Maria, joke about drinking and revelry. They make fun of Sir Toby's friend, Sir Andrew Aguecheek, who is staying with them, ostensibly to woo Olivia but really to fund Sir Toby's drinking.

Orsino decides to send 'Cesario' (Viola) as a messenger to Olivia's house to convey his love. However, by this time Viola has fallen in love with Orsino. Feste, Olivia's fool/jester, jokes with Olivia, but her steward, Malvolio, disapproves of Feste's riddles, calling him a 'barren rascal' (1.5.67). When Viola arrives, asking to speak with Olivia, Malvolio tries to send her away, but Olivia, intrigued, agrees to see 'Cesario'. Viola describes Orsino's passionate feelings, but Olivia instead becomes interested in Cesario and, when Viola leaves, sends Malvolio after 'him' with a ring. Viola realises that Olivia now has feelings for Cesario, making her situation even more difficult.

Sebastian, Viola's twin brother, has also arrived in Illyria, along with another sea captain, Antonio. Though Antonio is devoted to (and perhaps in love with) Sebastian, they part ways because Antonio knows his past in Illyria puts him in danger of arrest by Orsino's men.

Sir Toby and Sir Andrew party deep into the night, waking Maria and then Malvolio, who rebukes them for having 'no wit, manners, nor honesty' (2.3.75–6). Sir Toby defends his right to a life of pleasure, and Maria sides with him, declaring Malvolio 'a puritan ... an affectioned ass' (2.3.124–5); she vows to play a trick on him.

Orsino and Viola discuss love, especially unrequited love. Viola indirectly describes her feelings for Orsino, but because he believes her to be a man he does not make the connection, and she agrees to go to Olivia's once again.

Sir Toby, Sir Andrew and Fabian (another member of Olivia's household) hide and watch as Malvolio finds what appears to be a love letter from Olivia (actually written by Maria). Thinking his dreams are about to come true, Malvolio takes the letter at face value and plans to dress as the letter describes: 'in yellow stockings and cross-gartered' (2.5.141–2). It is clear to all (including the audience) that Malvolio will look ridiculous; Maria and Sir Toby can hardly wait to see him humiliated.

Viola and Olivia have a long conversation, at the end of which Olivia confesses her feelings. Viola comes close to revealing her own truth, but in the end simply promises to stop bringing her 'master's tears' (3.1.147) to Olivia.

Continuing the pranks, Sir Toby convinces Sir Andrew that Cesario now stands between him and Olivia's affections, and that Sir Andrew should challenge the young man to a duel.

Sebastian and Antonio reach the town, and Antonio reiterates his fear of arrest. He gives Sebastian his purse and goes to find lodgings for the evening.

Meanwhile, Malvolio dresses according to the letter's advice, but Olivia is bewildered and concerned for his wellbeing. Sir Toby decides to continue the prank and place Malvolio (still unaware he is being tricked) in a dark room on the pretext that he really is mad. Sir Andrew has written a letter challenging Cesario, but neither he nor Viola really wish to fight. Nevertheless, urged on by Sir Toby, they draw their swords – only for Antonio to arrive and defend 'Cesario', who he thinks is Sebastian. Antonio is then arrested, and is upset when 'Sebastian' refuses to return his purse.

The real Sebastian is found by Sir Andrew and Sir Toby, who think he is Cesario and begin a fight. Olivia arrives, dismisses them and takes Sebastian to her house; he promises (though wondering if he is dreaming) to be 'ruled' by her (4.1.57).

Malvolio is visited in his cell by 'Sir Topas' – Feste in disguise as a curate (clergyman). Malvolio refuses to believe he is mad, realising how cruelly he has been treated. He asks for paper and ink to write to Olivia.

Olivia and Sebastian (who she believes is Cesario) exchange vows in her private chapel. When Orsino and Viola arrive at her house, Olivia is confused by Cesario's loyalty to Orsino and calls Cesario 'husband' (5.1.132), angering Orsino. The tension is only relieved by the entrances of Sir Toby and Sir Andrew, both injured in a fight with Sebastian, and then Sebastian himself. Everyone is amazed at the likeness between Sebastian and Viola, each of whom is astonished to find the other alive. Viola reveals her true identity, and Orsino promises to marry her.

Finally, Olivia is shown the love letter found by Malvolio and she identifies it as being written by Maria, revealing the trick against her loyal steward. Fabian and Feste plead for tolerance and understanding, with Feste recalling Malvolio's 'barren rascal' insult (5.1.353), but Malvolio refuses to be placated, vowing to have his revenge. Feste concludes with a melancholy song, tempering the play's wit and energy with an acknowledgement of life's hardships.

Character summaries

Viola (disguised as 'Cesario' for most of the play)

Viola and her near-identical twin Sebastian are separated in a shipwreck some time after their father's death, and arrive in Illyria, neither knowing the other is alive. Viola disguises herself as a young man to protect herself and secure employment. As Cesario, a page serving Orsino (whom she falls in love with), she is sent to Olivia to convey Orsino's love, but Olivia falls in love with Cesario. When Viola and Sebastian are reunited and her true identity is revealed, Viola and Orsino become engaged.

Olivia

The Countess Olivia's father and brother have recently died, leaving her a single woman in possession of wealth and property. Initially she is reclusive and rejects Orsino's ongoing courtship; but, captivated by Viola (as Cesario), she proposes – though, unwittingly, to Sebastian, whom she welcomes as a husband when Viola's disguise is revealed.

Orsino

A wealthy duke (or count – he is described as both), Orsino is initially in love with Olivia. However, he is drawn to Cesario and, when the twins' true identities are revealed, becomes engaged to Viola.

Maria

Maria is a gentlewoman (a woman who attends upon an upper-class woman) in Olivia's household. She sets out to punish Malvolio for his priggishness, writing a letter to make him believe that Olivia loves him. Maria later (offstage) marries Sir Toby, though she seems exasperated by his and Sir Andrew's drunken behaviour rather than fond of him.

Feste

A professional jester/fool in Olivia's court, Feste entertains with jokes, songs and riddles in exchange for payment. He participates in the trick against Malvolio by pretending to be Sir Topas the curate, sent to Malvolio to assess his state of mind.

Sir Toby Belch

Sir Toby, Olivia's uncle, is a long-term house guest who takes advantage of his niece's hospitality. He spends evenings in drunken revelry with his friend Sir Andrew, whom he has invited to Olivia's court to woo her and to supply money and alcohol. He collaborates in the trick against Malvolio, and also unkindly deceives Sir Andrew into fighting Cesario. Sir Toby marries Maria.

Sir Andrew Aguecheek

A friend of Sir Toby's, Sir Andrew is foolish and poorly suited to Olivia, whom he is ostensibly courting. He joins in with Maria and Sir Toby's plans and jokes but is generally ineffectual.

Malvolio

Malvolio, Olivia's steward responsible for her household, values order and propriety. He is disliked by Maria and Sir Toby for being pompous and overly strict, and for having a high opinion of himself (he imagines he could marry Olivia). He is easily deceived by the letter Maria writes and is humiliated and persecuted when he obeys the instructions in it.

Sebastian

Viola's twin makes his way to the same part of Illyria some time after her, having kept company with the sea captain Antonio. Because Viola has been living in Illyria dressed as a young man, people Sebastian meets (including Feste, Sir Toby and Olivia) all assume Sebastian is Cesario, causing much confusion. Sebastian agrees unhesitatingly when Olivia proposes (believing he is Cesario), and he and Viola are reunited in the final scene.

Antonio

A sea captain who survives the shipwreck, Antonio rescues then supports Sebastian, whom he adores. Past conflicts in Illyria put him at risk when he shows his face there, and he is eventually arrested.

BACKGROUND & CONTEXT

Twelfth Night

Some Shakespeare scholars believe that *Twelfth Night* was written to be performed for Queen Elizabeth I to celebrate Twelfth Night in 1601 or 1602. Twelfth Night marks the end of the twelve days of Christmas, beginning on Christmas Day (25 December) and ending on 5 January. Historically it was a festive occasion with its origins in older traditions that had no connection with Christianity. In the Roman tradition of Saturnalia, for example, masters and servants could swap roles and one man was appointed king for a day. A similar tradition in England involved a Lord of Misrule – someone from the lower classes who was selected to be in charge of the revelries. Heavy drinking featured, but just as important was freedom from the usual conventions and constraints.

These elements of festivity and revelry are evident in *Twelfth Night* as Sir Toby resists Malvolio's attempts to impose order and propriety, instead creating disorder and mayhem. In the early scenes of the play Olivia is relatively absent from the affairs of the household, while Malvolio, the steward, is treated with contempt by Sir Toby, Sir Andrew, Maria and Feste.

Boy actors on the Elizabethan stage

During Shakespeare's lifetime (in fact, up until the 1660s), it was against the law for women to act on stage. Instead, female roles were played by boys and young men, usually between the ages of twelve and twenty-one. The boy actors were generally apprenticed to more senior male actors in companies such as the Lord Chamberlain's Men. (They had a different status to the boy performers often attached to choir schools, who performed but were not in training for adult roles.) Most companies probably had up to five boy actors; they were paid less than the adult actors but still became very accomplished performers. (Demanding and complex Shakespearean female roles such as Juliet and Cleopatra confirm this.) The role of Viola, like all Shakespeare's female characters, would have been performed by a boy actor, probably around sixteen or seventeen years old. This adds an extra dimension to her gender disguise when she performs the 'male' role of Cesario.

Many scholars have questioned how Shakespearean audiences would have viewed the boy actors: 'Did spectators accept the convention, ignore the boy actor's gender, read him as her?' (Hodgdon 2002, p.187). While we cannot know for sure how these performances were 'read' at the time, eyewitness accounts of Elizabethan or Jacobean performances provide clues; for example, some write about the female characters without reference to the male actors (Hodgdon 2002). However, it probably wasn't as simple as that: there was bound to be some awareness of the 'performance' taking place, the contrast between the actor's underlying sex and the gender being represented. Hodgdon also notes that modern audiences tend to 'import' (p.187) their own conventions and expectations to Shakespeare's texts, making it harder for us to imagine earlier understandings of the complexities of gender representation. Other commentators note that there was likely a contradiction inherent in the interpretation of sex and gender on stage: there was likely 'a high level of awareness by audiences of the presence of play-boys in female roles' while simultaneously 'English theatergoers seem to have accepted boys in women's parts as the norm of theatrical representation' (Shapiro 1995, p.41).

We can certainly assume, though, that when Orsino catalogues the ways in which Cesario is so like a woman (1.4.30–3), or when Malvolio describes Cesario as 'not yet old enough for a man, nor young enough for a boy' (1.5.130), an Elizabethan audience had a different experience of this three-layered 'joke' than we would have now if watching a female actor playing Viola. Remember, too, that these complexities are more apparent for viewers, with the physical reminder of the boy-actor's body, than for readers, where the script foregrounds the *character's* sex (rather than the actor's), using 'Viola' rather than 'Cesario' at the beginning of lines.

Settings

Illyria is an old name for the area on the eastern coast of the Adriatic Sea – a region now known as the countries of Albania and Montenegro, to the north of Greece. On the western coast of the Adriatic is Italy. Sebastian tells Antonio that he and Viola are from Messaline (2.1.12), an imaginary place that sounds like it could be Italian. In other words, Sebastian and Viola are not all that far from home, but are in unfamiliar territory where no one knows who they are, giving them freedom to redefine themselves.

Despite this exotic location, much of the setting would have felt familiar to Shakespeare's audiences. In Act 3, Scene 3, Antonio recommends that Sebastian stays at 'the Elephant' (3.3.39), an allusion to the Oliphant, a London inn not far from the Globe Theatre, where Shakespeare's plays were often performed.

The stately houses of Orsino and Olivia are also evocative of English manors and palaces. Olivia's estate has extensive gardens, suggested by phrases such as 'let the garden door be shut' (3.1.78) and Viola's 'make me a willow cabin at your gate' (1.5.223). Her instruction to Sebastian to 'go with me ... / Into the chantry by' (4.3.23–4) indicates she has a private chapel, another sign of land and privilege. Both Olivia's and Orsino's courts are large enough to accommodate servants, and Olivia's houses guests with whom she rarely interacts, even though they stay for months.

GENRE, STRUCTURE & LANGUAGE

Genre

Twelfth Night is a Shakespearean comedy. Although this implies a play with abundant humour – which *Twelfth Night* certainly has – the genre is more complex. Shakespeare's comedies typically follow the romantic journeys of two or more protagonists encountering various tests and challenges including misunderstandings, mistaken identities and miscommunications; disguises and transformations often play a role. In the end, truths are revealed and two or more marriages take place (or are imminent). All these generic features are evident in *Twelfth Night*.

Whereas Shakespeare's tragedies depict the end of a social order, his comedies depict renewal and regeneration. As a result of being shipwrecked, Sebastian and Viola have temporarily lost their place in society. They are outsiders in Illyria, and must establish relationships and social status. Similarly, the connection between Orsino and Olivia has broken down so completely at the start of the play that Orsino is compelled to send a messenger to convey his feelings, while Olivia has renounced 'the sight / And company of men' (1.2.40–1). By the end of the play, though, both have found loving companions and Olivia invites Orsino to 'think me as well a sister as a wife' (5.1.296).

The many sources of humour in the play include Feste's sparring word play with Olivia, Orsino and Viola, and the drunken antics of Sir Toby and Sir Andrew, which, at least until Act 2, Scene 3, appear foolish but relatively harmless. In performance, physical comedy can enhance the verbal humour. However, the play also explores and evokes many other moods, including melancholy (as when Orsino and Viola contemplate unrequited love), and a sense of wonder and pathos (as in the final scene). While the pompous Malvolio is a source of amusement for the audience as well as for his companions, Sir Toby and Maria's treatment of him tips over into maliciousness in Act 2, Scene 5, leading the audience to feel less comfortable about their laughter.

Structure

Twelfth Night is structured by its three parallel plot lines:

- the love triangle involving Viola, Orsino and Olivia
- Sebastian and Antonio navigating an unfamiliar and, for Antonio, hostile society
- the revelry of Sir Toby, Sir Andrew, Maria and Fabian, and their tormenting of Malvolio.

The three plot lines interweave, gradually coming together. In Act 3, Scene 4, Sir Toby convinces Cesario and Sir Andrew to duel, and then Antonio intervenes; Sebastian enters Olivia's world in Act 4, Scene 1. Feste plays a vital role connecting the characters and the narrative threads, moving easily between the households of Olivia and Orsino, and also between the 'lower' characters (e.g. Sir Toby and Sir Andrew) and the 'higher' characters (Olivia, Orsino, Viola and Sebastian) on whom he depends for payment. The characters are not all together on stage until the single scene of Act 5, when the three plot lines merge and, to use Viola's metaphor, the complexities are 'untangled'.

The play is also structured according to the conventions of comedy: the main characters encounter obstacles and conflict, leading to a decline in their fortunes. Viola reaches perhaps her lowest point when she is forced to draw her sword to defend herself against Sir Andrew (Act 3, Scene 4), and is saved only by the fortuitous arrival of Antonio. Although this leads temporarily to further conflict when Antonio mistakes her for Sebastian and pleads for his purse, this scene signals a turning point in Viola's fortunes when Antonio refers to her brother.

In the end, Sebastian and Viola are reunited, most sources of conflict are resolved and the play concludes joyously. However, positive emotions are balanced by Malvolio's powerful sense of injustice and Feste's cautionary song about the 'wind and rain' (5.1.366–85), a reminder of life's unending challenges.

Imagery

Several patterns of imagery run through *Twelfth Night*, helping to convey characters' emotions and attitudes, and contributing to the play's exploration of wider issues and ideas, including truth, love, madness, time and fate.

Light versus dark

The characters' attempts to locate the truth in strange, confusing times, when they are tempted to doubt their own sanity, are often mirrored by images of light and dark. Sebastian initially feels that the 'stars shine darkly over me' (2.1.2), but after meeting Olivia he breathes in 'the air, that is the glorious sun' (4.3.1) – love, in other words, dispels the darkness and brings in the light and warmth of the sun.

Darkness is aligned with madness, or at least the absence of reason and knowledge. In an attempt to convince Malvolio that he is truly mad, Sir Toby decides that they will put him 'in a dark room and bound' (3.4.114); Malvolio protests against the 'hideous darkness' (4.2.25). Feste (as Sir Topas) compounds the manipulation, telling Malvolio 'there is no darkness but ignorance' (4.2.34). Malvolio responds with 'this house is as dark as ignorance' (4.2.36), an observation that resonates with the kinds of ignorance evident in Olivia's long-term house guests. In Act 5, Malvolio's letter to Olivia provides evidence that he has indeed retained his sanity:

> Though you have put me into darkness ... yet have I the benefit of my senses as well as your ladyship. (5.1.283–5)

Only in the final act do light and sense replace the darkness and confusion pervading the play. Olivia had intended to keep her exchange of vows with Sebastian 'in darkness' (5.1.142), but summons the priest to reveal their secret ceremony; Viola refers to 'that orbèd continent the fire' (the sun) that 'severs day from night' (5.1.255–6) as a symbol of truth.

Sea and water imagery

Despite Viola and Sebastian surviving a shipwreck, imagery of drowning and immersion pervades the play. Viola is convinced Sebastian has gone 'to his wat'ry tomb' (5.1.218), while Sebastian is certain that Viola 'is drowned already' and that his tears will 'drown her remembrance again with more' (2.1.22–3). He echoes this line in Act 5 with 'I should my tears let fall upon your cheek' (5.1.224), though at this point the twins restrain their emotions rather than becoming subsumed by them.

Orsino's language connects the sea not with death but with love. His simile describes the 'spirit of love' that 'receiveth as the sea'; it is 'quick and fresh' (1.1.9–11), thus aligning the sea – and love – with change and mutability. Love, then, is volatile, perhaps signalling the eventual transfer of Orsino's devotion from Olivia to Viola. Yet love is also consuming; Orsino's passion is 'as hungry as the sea' (2.4.96).

Other characters, faced with circumstances defying normal boundaries and mores, are akin to vessels adrift at sea, trying to navigate to calmer waters. Feste jokes that Sir Andrew stays 'o'th'windy side of the law' (3.4.139), comparing him to a sailor steering into the wind to remain safe from the rocky shore. Maria asks Cesario to 'hoist sail', but Viola insists she will 'hull here a little longer' (1.5.166–7).

Trapping and hunting

A network of images alludes to ideas of trapping and hunting. Most obviously, Malvolio and Sir Andrew are 'gulled', meaning deceived: Maria vows to 'gull' Malvolio (2.3.114); Fabian calls her his 'noble gull-catcher' (2.5.154); Sir Toby's final insult to Sir Andrew is to call him 'a gull' (5.1.191).

Numerous references to hunting and catching birds include Sir Toby's 'now is the woodcock near the gin' (2.5.69; a 'gin' is a trap) and Malvolio's 'I have limed her' (3.4.66; lime was a sticky substance used to ensnare birds). Maria uses a fishing metaphor when she anticipates Malvolio discovering her letter: 'here comes the trout that must be caught with tickling' (2.5.18–19). Sir Toby calls Maria 'the youngest wren of mine' (3.2.52), signalling that he intends to capture her – though their compatibility is evident and Maria's willingness to be thus ensnared is implied by their mutual enjoyment of Malvolio's humiliation.

Riddles and puns

Like most of Shakespeare's fools, Feste usually speaks in riddles that contain insights and truths. Unlike the jokes of Sir Toby and Sir Andrew, Feste's word play shows him to be a sharp observer of those around him, and both Olivia and Orsino pay attention to his chatter – and pay him, too.

The exchanges between Olivia and Viola often have this riddling quality, such as when Viola says, 'I am not what I am' and Olivia responds, 'I would you were as I would have you be' (3.1.126–7). Viola speaks the truth, though in a way only the audience completely grasps; Olivia does too, though without realising it. They speak in paradoxes that both hide and reveal the truth about their feelings and identities. In the end, the characters speak plainly to one another; but for most of the play, riddles and puns create a world in which nothing is quite certain.

Names

Several of the characters' names are suggestive, connecting them to central concerns in the play. 'Feste', for example, connotes 'festivity', linking with the revelry of Sir Toby (in which Feste joins in Act 2, Scene 3) and the idea of Twelfth Night being a time of misrule. Feste's riddles, jokes and puns also make his name apt.

The similarity of 'Viola' and 'Olivia' (they are nearly anagrams) points to a connection between the two characters. At the start of the play each is mourning a brother and has lost a father; both are in charge of their own destinies; and by the end of the play they are soon to become sisters (by marriage), connected through Sebastian. More intriguingly, the name 'Malvolio' also has similarities with 'Viola' and 'Olivia' – though his character seems diametrically opposite to theirs.

The name 'Malvolio' links, through the prefix 'mal' (bad, wrongful), to words such as 'malign' and 'malevolent'. However, in a sign that names don't necessarily truly reflect personality, he is in some ways a benign character, loyal to Olivia and trying to impose some order on an unruly household. Similarly, the knighthoods of 'Sir' Toby and 'Sir' Andrew suggest status and respectability, but the two men lack compassion and integrity. The name 'Maria' connotes the Virgin Mary, a figure synonymous with purity and virtue, whereas unkind Maria is eager to see Malvolio humiliated. Sir Toby's surname, 'Belch', accurately connotes his love of eating and drinking, while the name 'topas', adopted by Feste when pretending to be a curate, is ironic; the gemstone topaz was 'believed to have a curative effect on madness' (Davis & Frankforter 2004, p.487). 'Sir Topas', of course, sets out to have the opposite effect on Malvolio.

Music

Music (the second word spoken in the play) has an important role in *Twelfth Night*, often reinforcing the play's festive elements. Music accompanies the opening lines, and concludes the play, in Feste's song. The director of any performance can influence the audience's responses to the action and characters through the emotional qualities of the music performed.

Twelfth Night has more songs than is typical for an early-seventeenth-century play. Some have speculated this may be partly because it was written for a special occasion, possibly performed away from the Globe Theatre (where musical resources would have been fairly limited), thus allowing Shakespeare to write more music into the script (Springfels 2015). Shakespeare is known for having both penned his own songs and made use of existing melodies and lyrics.

Sometimes the songs appear to be purely for entertainment, but they can also provide additional layers of meaning. In Act 2, Scene 3, for example, Feste joins the drunken partying with a song ('O mistress mine, where are you roaming?', from l.33) that treats the subject of love in a lighthearted fashion, matching the carefree nature of the party. Yet it takes on additional meaning through possible reference to Olivia, and its advice to make the most of present love since 'what's to come is still unsure' (l.43). There might also be a link to Viola and Sebastian, in Olivia's 'true love … that can sing both high and low' (l.35) – a possible reference to their female and male voices.

Feste's song in Act 2, Scene 4 has a far more melancholy tone, again matching the scene's mood, which is reflective and sombre. The line 'come away, come away, death' (l.49), and the song's portrayal of a young man despondent due to unrequited love, accords with Viola's image of her father's daughter who 'sat like Patience on a monument, / Smiling at grief' (l.110–11). The song deepens the mood as Orsino and Viola confide their feelings, even if Viola continues to keep her biggest secret to herself.

Like a number of Shakespeare's comedies, *Twelfth Night* ends with a character directly addressing the audience but, in this case, the address is in the form of a song. Accompanying the so-called happy endings experienced by most of the main characters, Feste's song is somewhat dark, including references to ceaseless rain and phrases such as 'never thrive' (5.1.376). This gives weight to Malvolio's lack of resolution, and leaves the audience considering the bleaker sides of the story. However, as the original music for these songs is lost, the lyrics can be interpreted differently by individual directors. For example, the song's downbeat lyrics could be juxtaposed against an upbeat tempo. Alternatively, the music chosen could emphasise the melancholy of the lyrics, offsetting the play's comic and romantic elements.

SCENE-BY-SCENE ANALYSIS

Act 1

1.1 Summary: *Duke Orsino declares that he is in love with Olivia, who is in mourning for her brother and refuses to see anyone.*

The short opening scene introduces the lovesick Orsino. His poetic language, rich in imagery, suggests a lively imagination and strong feelings; later, Viola's ability to match him in conversation signals their compatibility.

Sea imagery also suggests a link between Orsino and Viola. Orsino compares the 'spirit of love' (l.9) to the sea in its capacity to absorb elements, which then fall 'into abatement' (l.13). On a simple reading, Orsino is merely saying that his affections might rise and fall, just as the music, initially pleasing, has lost its appeal. But a 'dying fall' (l.4) and the image of the sea that 'receiveth' (l.11) resonate with the idea of drowning, which is central to the next scene.

Q What is your initial impression of Orsino?

1.2. Summary: *Viola and a sea captain are shipwrecked on the coast of Illyria. Viola despairs that her brother, Sebastian, has drowned, and decides to disguise herself and seek employment in Orsino's court.*

Although Viola believes Sebastian is probably dead – in 'Elysium' (l.4), a blessed form of the afterlife in Greek mythology – the Captain's account of him clinging to 'a strong mast' for 'so long as I could see' (l.14, l.17) suggests he has survived, preparing the audience for Sebastian's appearance in Act 2.

The Captain has a minor role in the play as a whole, but in this scene he provides important background information, naming the location, Illyria, and identifying both Orsino and Olivia – 'a noble duke' (l.25) and 'a virtuous maid, the daughter of a count' (l.36) – as members of the nobility, worthy of respect.

Key point

While in Scene 1 Orsino indulges in an excess of feeling, wanting more music to provoke more love, here Olivia represents extreme restraint. The Captain's description of her 'abjur[ing] the sight / And company of men' (1.2.40–1) confirms the impression Valentine (one of Orsino's attendants) has of her as 'like a cloistress' (1.1.28) – a nun. This tension between excess and restraint runs through the play, with only the unions at the end bringing moderation and balance.

Viola imagines she wouldn't be accepted by Olivia, and can't safely join Orsino's court as a woman, so she decides to disguise herself as 'an eunuch' (l.56), a castrated male servant who typically guarded the women in a royal court – although she is regarded as a young male page (not a eunuch) by all who meet her.

Q Viola asserts that 'nature with a beauteous wall / Doth oft close in pollution' (l.48–9), believing that attractive appearances often hide bad behaviour or intentions. To what extent do later events of the play support this view?

1.3 Summary: *In Olivia's household, Maria, Sir Toby and Sir Andrew reveal their love of revelry.*

While much of the play's action concerns the love triangle between Orsino, Olivia and Viola, the interactions of Maria, Sir Toby, Sir Andrew and the other members of Olivia's household form an important subplot. Like Orsino and Viola in the previous scenes, they like to play with language, but their banter is entirely different from the poetry of their social superiors. These characters are not members of the nobility, but are dependent on them for employment and sustenance. Maria is a gentlewoman who performs various domestic duties for Olivia, while Sir Toby, a relative of Olivia, seems determined to remain in the house, doing little of value and indulging in food and wine regularly.

In contrast to the poetry used in earlier scenes, these characters' lines are written as prose. This is typical in Shakespearean drama: prose is often used for the lower-class characters, and verse for those of higher social rank. There are other contrasts, too. While Orsino's elevated language explores love and beauty, Sir Toby's is geared to bodily pleasures, signalled by his assertion that his clothes are 'good enough to drink in' (l.9) and the ribald (sexually charged) undertone of his explanation of the word 'accost': 'front her, board her, woo her, assail her' (l.46–7). Maria's gentle plea that he remain 'within the modest limits of order' (l.6–7) only emphasises the unlikelihood of that happening.

Q Although Sir Toby greets Sir Andrew with some affection, what signs are there in this scene that he considers Sir Andrew someone he can manipulate and mock?

1.4 Summary: *Viola, disguised as Cesario, has rapidly earned Orsino's trust; he tasks her with relaying his love to Olivia. In an aside, Viola confesses her love for Orsino.*

In just three days, Viola has become accepted and highly regarded in Orsino's court. Orsino predicts that Olivia will listen to Cesario, though his reasoning is interesting: he emphasises not only the virtues of Cesario's youth (l.26) but also 'his' feminine qualities. He compares Cesario's 'smooth and rubious' lips to those of Diana (goddess of the hunt, and of fertility) and describes 'his' voice as like 'the maiden's organ, shrill and sound' (l.31–2). Viola is disguised as a young man, yet has some physical traits of a young woman. This gender ambiguity is a feature of Viola/Cesario and is, in part, what enables her to move easily between the courts of Orsino and Olivia.

The aside that ends this short scene establishes another side of the love triangle that runs through the play. Orsino is in love with Olivia, and Viola is secretly in love with Orsino. Soon Olivia will meet, and fall in love with, 'Cesario' (Viola).

Q Orsino tells Cesario to 'be clamorous, and leap all civil bounds' (l.20). Does Viola follow Orsino's instructions, or does she find her own way to connect with Olivia?

1.5 Summary: *The fool Feste talks wittily with Maria, Olivia and Malvolio. Olivia is told 'a young gentleman' (l.81) wishes to speak to her; she refuses, but then becomes curious and eventually agrees. After Viola leaves, Olivia confesses her affection for Cesario, and sends Malvolio after 'him' with a ring.*

This scene introduces three central characters: Feste, Malvolio and Olivia. Both Maria and Olivia engage with Feste's word play, but Malvolio shows his distaste for Feste and his banter. He calls Feste a 'barren rascal' (l.67), and Olivia mildly rebukes him for taking things too seriously – she approves of being 'generous, guiltless, and of free disposition' (l.74–5), a sign that, despite her intention to withdraw from society, she has an essentially kind and open nature.

This exchange also highlights Malvolio's difference from those around him: he is earnest and often sanctimonious, and his speech lacks the frequent metaphors and puns of the others. His observations of Cesario, though, echo Orsino's language in the previous scene, indicating that he can be astute and perceptive. He describes Cesario as 'between boy and man' (l.132), capturing some of the ambiguity of Viola/Cesario. He also notes that Cesario says, 'he'll stand at your door like a sheriff's post' (l.122–3) – Viola is clearly following Orsino's instruction to 'stand at her doors, / And tell them there thy fixèd foot shall grow' (1.4.15–16).

As Viola and Olivia talk, their language shifts from prose to poetry, and they engage more closely with each other. At first, Olivia is blunt and direct – 'Whence came you, sir?' (l.147) – while Viola is more mannered and stagey: 'good swabber, I am to hull here a little longer' (l.167). Gradually, though, Olivia's speech becomes more relaxed, and Viola even hints at her underlying reality: 'What I am, and what I would, are as secret as maidenhead' (l.177–8). She entices Olivia to remove her veil, and her description of Olivia's beauty (when her lines shift into poetry for the first time, l.195–9) is expressive and sincere. Olivia, too, begins to speak in verse, showing her eloquence and grace as she describes Orsino (l.213–17).

In this section, Olivia and Viola sometimes respond to each other so promptly that they complete each other's ten-syllable lines of iambic pentameter (see the explanation of blank verse on page 68 of this text guide). For example:

> Viola: But you should pity me!
> Olivia: You might do much. (l.231)

However, Viola is unable to move past Olivia's insistence that she 'cannot love him' (l.235), and she leaves abruptly, rejecting Olivia's offer of money ('keep your purse', l.239) and accusing Olivia of heartlessness: 'Farewell, fair cruelty' (l.243).

Yet Olivia's short soliloquy shows how quickly she has been captivated by Cesario. She sends Malvolio after Cesario with a ring, hoping to influence the course of events, but she admits that fate will 'show' its 'force' (l.265). While Orsino wants to try everything – 'to leap all civil bounds' (1.4.20) – to convince Olivia to love him, Olivia is more accepting of what will unfold. In this she echoes Viola's sentiment at the end of Scene 2: 'What else may hap, to time I will commit' (1.2.60), reinforcing the connection between the two women.

Q What are your impressions of Olivia in this scene? In what ways does she conform to the earlier descriptions of her (e.g. the Captain's at 1.2.36–41), and in what ways does she differ?

Act 2

2.1 Summary: *Viola's brother, Sebastian, and the sea captain Antonio talk briefly as they go their separate ways; Antonio reveals his love for Sebastian and the danger he faces in Illyria from Orsino's men.*

This scene mirrors Act 1, Scene 2: Antonio, like Viola's companion, is a sea captain, and Sebastian praises his 'excellent … touch of modesty' (l.8) just as Viola praised her captain's 'fair behaviour' (1.2.47). Sebastian fears that his sister has drowned, just as she feared the same of him. However, Antonio's evident feelings for Sebastian, and Sebastian's insistence that they part, give this scene a very different quality.

There is also an echo of the previous scene, in which Olivia declares her feelings for 'Cesario' (although admittedly not knowing that they are both women). Antonio's admission in the short soliloquy that ends the scene – 'I do adore thee' (l.35) – is a more explicit acknowledgement of a same-sex attraction.

2.2 Summary: *Malvolio tries to give Cesario the ring from Olivia, but Viola refuses to accept it. In a soliloquy, she spells out the love triangle that has developed, and despairs of finding a solution.*

Malvolio shows how loyal he is to Olivia, following her commands and ensuring that Cesario knows he can return to 'report' (l.8) how Orsino takes Olivia's rejection. The idea that Cesario left a ring is an invention of Olivia's, but Malvolio extends the story, insisting that Cesario 'peevishly threw it to her' (l.11). After he leaves, Viola admits her puzzlement – 'I left no ring with her' (l.14) – but she is even more concerned by Olivia's feelings, and the fact that her own disguise has potentially caused unhappiness: 'Disguise, I see thou art a wickedness' (l.24).

Key point

Again, the idea of false appearances is raised, but this time Viola is aware that the deception is of her own doing. As a man she has led Olivia to fall in love with her, and as a woman disguised as a man she is unable to express her feelings for Orsino.

Viola appeals to time once more to solve her problems, using the metaphor of a knot:

> O time, thou must untangle this, not I;
> It is too hard a knot for me t'untie. (l.37–8)

This 'knot' only becomes more difficult for Viola to 'untie', especially once Sebastian becomes caught up in events, but, as in most comedies, the final scene of the play does indeed disentangle the various misunderstandings and enable the couples to be happily paired off.

Q To what extent do you think Viola is responsible for the difficult position she finds herself in? Do you agree with her view that 'our frailty is the cause ... such as we are made of, such we be' (l.28–9)?

2.3 Summary: *Sir Toby and Sir Andrew drink into the early hours of the morning; Feste joins them, and their singing draws Maria and then Malvolio into the room. Malvolio rebukes the men, but leaves. His high-handed manner annoys the revellers, and Maria plans to trick Malvolio by writing love letters seemingly from Olivia.*

This scene – sometimes called the 'kitchen scene' by critics, as it is assumed that is where the nightly drinking would have taken place – shows Sir Toby, Sir Andrew and Feste at their most carefree and high-spirited. In contrast, Malvolio is at his most indignant and puritanical. Indeed, Maria calls him 'a kind of puritan' (l.119), referring to a strict religious group in the early seventeenth century that opposed most forms of entertainment, including theatrical performances. However, there is no strong evidence that Malvolio actually is a Puritan, and much of what he says to Sir Toby is not unreasonable. He accuses them of having 'no wit, manners, nor honesty' and of making 'an alehouse of my lady's house', with no 'respect of place, persons, nor time' (l.75–9). Sir Toby is indeed exploiting his relative's kindness – by the end of the play he will have been in the house for at least three months (5.1.83) – and only tolerates Sir Andrew as a source of amusement and funds (he insists that Sir Andrew 'send for money', l.156).

Unlike Malvolio, Sir Toby embodies a hedonistic approach to life, taking pleasure where and as often as he can. He does not object to others not sharing his values, but he does object to Malvolio trying to dictate how he lives: 'Dost thou think because thou art virtuous there shall be no more cakes and ale?' (l.97–9).

Key point

Beneath the guise of comedy lies a serious debate about the role of moderation in life. Sir Toby lives to excess, but it could be argued that Malvolio does, too – an excess of seriousness and self-denial that seems to preclude happiness. Somewhere, the play suggests, lies a happy medium between these opposing tendencies.

Although Maria at first tries to moderate the revellers' behaviour ('what a caterwauling do you keep here!', l.63), she resents Malvolio's intrusion and vows to 'gull him' (l.114). Her assertion that she can write 'very like my lady ... we can hardly make distinction of our hands' (l.134–6) may be an exaggeration, since in the end Olivia has no difficulty in recognising Maria's handwriting (5.1.326). However, Maria is encouraged by the two men, particularly Sir Toby. By this point, they feel they can get away with anything: Sir Toby, the Lord of Misrule, is in full flight.

Q Malvolio's question, 'My masters, are you mad?' (l.75), is one of many references in the play to madness. Later, Malvolio himself is accused of being mad. In this scene, who seems to behave as if they have lost touch with their sanity? Who acts reasonably?

2.4 Summary: *Orsino and Viola discuss love and life; Feste sings a melancholy song about unrequited love.*

This scene finds Orsino in a reflective mood, asking for 'but one verse' of an 'old and antique song' to 'relieve [his] passion' (l.3–7). In Feste's song of a metaphorical death from a broken heart, the 'fair cruel maid' (l.52) mirrors Orsino's conception of Olivia.

Before and after the song, though, Orsino and Viola discuss their own loves. Viola has to disguise the true object of her affections, telling Orsino her love is 'of your complexion' and of 'about your years' (l.24, l.26), relying on Orsino's assumption that Cesario's love is a woman to hide the reality from him. The audience knows the truth, however, so Viola's cryptic responses serve to deepen their sympathy for her predicament.

Despite this prolonged misunderstanding, the poetic, melancholic language of both Orsino and Viola suggests a growing bond between them. When Viola obliquely describes her love for Orsino – 'My father had a daughter loved a man' (l.103) – he listens attentively, even as she challenges his assertion that a woman cannot love as intensely as a man. As in the exchanges between Viola and Olivia, in this conversation the lines of verse are often shared between Viola and Orsino. For example:

> Orsino: I cannot be so answered.
> Viola: Sooth, but you must. (l.84)

They don't always agree – Viola insists that women are 'as true of heart' (l.102) as men – and Viola's language is more restrained than Orsino's hyperbolic 'mine is all as hungry as the sea' (l.96), yet her description of 'Patience on a monument, / Smiling at grief' (l.110–11) conveys an equally intense feeling. The scene is only brought to an end when Viola changes the subject abruptly, asking, 'Sir, shall I to this lady?' (l.118), re-establishing the distance between them.

Q How does Viola's simile in the lines, 'She never told her love, / But let concealment like a worm i'th'bud / Feed on her damask cheek' (l.106–8) connect with other images that compare outward appearance and inner reality?

2.5 Summary: *Malvolio, thinking he is alone, confesses aloud his hope of becoming Olivia's husband and 'Count Malvolio'; Sir Toby, Sir Andrew and Fabian are concealed and mock Malvolio throughout the scene; Malvolio discovers Maria's letter and falls for the trick, believing it was written by Olivia.*

Malvolio's speech in the first part of this scene conveys his self-importance: he is, as Sir Toby says, 'an overweening rogue' (l.25), as he imagines himself 'three months married' to Olivia, enjoying a luxurious life in his 'branched velvet gown' (l.38, l.40). Yet the vindictiveness of those who seek to deceive him begins to test the audience's sympathies as Malvolio decides to win Olivia's affection by dressing 'in yellow stockings and cross-gartered' (l.141–2).

Maria declares she acts from 'the love of mockery' (l.15), but the effects of that mockery become clear by the end of the scene. Maria's calculation in knowing that yellow is 'a colour [Olivia] abhors' and that smiling at Olivia will 'turn [Malvolio] into a notable contempt' (l.166, l.169) shows her capacity for genuine cruelty. Sir Toby approves wholeheartedly, calling Maria a 'most excellent devil of wit' (l.170), and his line 'I could marry this wench for this device' (l.150) both reinforces their shared values and anticipates their eventual union.

Once again, the idea of madness is raised as Sir Toby predicts that Malvolio 'must run mad' (l.161). This is another instance of foreshadowing (although Malvolio's eventual 'madness' is more in others' estimation than in reality), and there is a sense of time unfolding to bring the plot's conflicts and complications to their just conclusions, as Viola has been hoping it will.

Sir Toby's antics have mainly been humorous to this point, but now the darker aspects of his character, and of the misrule he presides over, become more evident. As yet, though, he is blind to the sorry state in which he will end the play.

Q Dramatic irony results from the fact that the audience knows Malvolio's speech is overheard by Sir Toby, Sir Andrew and Fabian, and that the letter he thinks is from Olivia was written by Maria. To what extent does this create humour? Conversely, to what extent does it emphasise the malicious intent behind the trick, giving the scene a darker quality?

Act 3

3.1 Summary: *Feste talks to Cesario in riddles, earning two coins; Viola shares an extended dialogue with Olivia in which both come close to revealing truths.*

Viola shows her ability to move easily between places and language registers. In this she has a match in Feste, who is also able to move between the households of Olivia and Orsino, and to use his wit and linguistic flair to negotiate the world – and, as Viola's payments indicate, earn his living. Viola draws out Feste's wit and insights with a series of questions; her lines are in prose, just as they are in her exchange with Sir Toby and Sir Andrew, with whom she banters.

Once she and Olivia are in private, though, the dialogue reverts to verse. The final eighteen lines of the scene are in rhyming couplets, which are otherwise rare in the play (and generally only occur at the ends of scenes). The use of rhyme heightens the pathos of their exchange. They speak in riddles and paradoxes, skirting around truths:

> Olivia: I prithee tell me what thou think'st of me.
> Viola: That you do think you are not what you are.
> Olivia: If I think so, I think the same of you.
> Viola: Then think you right: I am not what I am.
> Olivia: I would you were as I would have you be. (I.123–7)

This rapid exchange of half-truths and confessions simultaneously keeps them apart and draws them together. Viola observes that Olivia is maintaining false appearances ('you are not what you are'), and Olivia recognises the same duplicity in Cesario, which Viola admits is true (she is, of course, a woman pretending to be a man). Olivia wishes for Cesario to be in love with her, a truth that Viola has already perceived, and the double meaning of Olivia's 'as I would have you be' is that she wishes (or she would, if she knew the truth) that Viola were really a man.

Eventually, Olivia confesses her love (the aside from line 130 can be taken to end at line 133, meaning Olivia is speaking to Cesario after this), bringing this truth into the open in a series of rhyming couplets. Viola replies, following Olivia's lead in her matching use of rhyming couplets, but she departs with her secrets intact.

Q At the end of this scene, Viola declares that 'never more / Will I my master's tears to you deplore' (I.146–7). Why do you think she decides not to convey Orsino's messages of love anymore?

3.2 Summary: *Fabian and Sir Toby trick Sir Andrew into believing Olivia is in love with him, and that he should challenge Cesario to a duel. Maria tells Sir Toby and Fabian to come and see Malvolio dressed in yellow stockings and cross-gartered.*

Sir Toby's manipulation of Sir Andrew continues, now aided by Fabian. This is another attempt to fool or 'gull' someone for amusement and, although Sir Andrew is not a very sympathetic character, the prospect of violence raises the stakes. Sir Toby's selfish aims are exposed when Fabian states plainly that Sir Andrew is 'a dear manikin' (l.42) – in other words, a puppet for Sir Toby – and when Sir Toby plays on the word 'dear' to refer to the 'two thousand' (l.43) that he has extracted from Sir Andrew (recall that at 1.3.18 Sir Toby said Sir Andrew 'has three thousand ducats a year').

The suggestion of violence in Sir Toby's insistence that Sir Andrew challenge 'the count's youth' and attempt to 'hurt him in eleven places' (l.27–8) is echoed when Maria anticipates, with apparent excitement, that Olivia 'will strike' Malvolio for smiling at her (l.64). The sense of order turning to disorder, of restraint being superseded by excess, is intensifying. Olivia's command over her household seems tenuous, as Sir Toby and Maria take control.

3.3 Summary: *Sebastian and Antonio arrive in the town; Antonio recalls a conflict with Orsino's men that makes him wish to remain out of sight.*

This short scene establishes some of the elements of the long, chaotic scene that follows. Antonio gives Sebastian his purse, an act that seems trivial but takes on greater significance in the next scene; Antonio emphasises the danger he faces if he is discovered ('if I be lapsèd in this place / I shall pay dear', l.36–7), which prepares the audience for his arrest.

3.4 Summary: *Malvolio appears before Olivia wearing yellow stockings, cross-gartered and smiling, leaving Olivia bewildered; Sir Andrew writes a letter challenging Cesario, but Sir Toby delivers the challenge in person; Viola does not want to fight, and even Sir Andrew suggests that* *they 'let the matter slip' (l.242), but Fabian and Sir Toby convince them to draw their swords; Antonio mistakes Viola for Sebastian, and also draws his sword; officers arrive and arrest Antonio, who is distressed at 'Sebastian' (Viola) not being able to return his purse.*

Near the end of this eventful scene, the 1st Officer declares, 'The time goes by' (l.315). The scene is a turning point in the play, when the passage of time begins to 'untangle' the 'knot' that has ensnared Viola, although at this stage things appear more confusing than ever. In many ways, this is Viola's lowest point in the play: she cannot return Olivia's feelings; she cannot make her own feelings known to Orsino; she is challenged to a pointless duel; she is accused by Antonio, whom she has never met, of having his purse. Yet Antonio calling her Sebastian gives her the first sign that her brother is still alive and that 'tempests are kind' (l.335).

Maria's plan comes to fruition as Malvolio follows the instructions of her letter, even quoting parts of it to Olivia to show his appreciation. It is a scene that can be very funny, but is, of course, completely humiliating for Malvolio. Olivia is baffled, but not, as Maria predicted, angry or violent; rather, she expresses sympathy and shows a generous, caring side to her character.

Sir Toby and Fabian continue to treat Sir Andrew as their 'manikin' (3.2.42), and extend their deceitfulness to Cesario, whom they draw into a potentially dangerous situation. In a series of blatant falsehoods, Sir Toby tells Cesario that Sir Andrew 'is a devil in private brawl' and so angry that 'satisfaction can be none but by pangs of death and sepulchre' (l.201–4). Viola displays characteristic restraint, seeking to negotiate rather than fight. By now, though, Sir Toby can think only of his amusement, and tells more lies to Sir Andrew, describing Cesario as a skilled fighter who 'will not now be pacified' (l.238). Sir Andrew wants to 'let the matter slip' (l.242) but Sir Toby insists the fight go ahead, demonstrating his loss of moral bearings. His inflated language – 'such a mortal motion' (l.234), 'perdition of souls' (l.245) – shows he has been carried away by his own rhetoric and imagination.

Fortunately, Antonio's arrival prevents the duel. Antonio again declares his love for Sebastian (Antonio is 'one … that for his love dares yet do more', l.268), making his confusion and distress when Viola is unable to return his purse more affecting. Viola's generosity in offering 'half [her] coffer' despite her 'lean and low ability' (l.297, l.294) is also moving; these are people who will give to others, whereas Sir Toby and his friends will only take.

Key point

When Antonio addresses Viola as Sebastian, he expresses his deep disappointment by accusing 'Sebastian' of being only 'the beauteous-evil' (l.320) – of having the appearance of beauty but not the reality. In other words, only what lies within can be genuinely admirable: 'virtue is beauty' (l.320). This echoes what Viola herself says to the Captain in Act 1 – 'nature with a beauteous wall / Doth oft close in pollution' (1.2.48–9) – reinforcing the play's message of valuing inner truths over external appearances.

The idea of madness is referenced by Antonio, whose misery threatens to make him 'so unsound a man' (l.301), and then by the 1st Officer ('the man grows mad', l.322). The chaos caused by the various disguises and schemes is reaching a climax, with the potential to cause genuine distress becoming more apparent.

Q Sir Toby calls Cesario 'a very dishonest paltry boy, and more a coward than a hare' (l.336). To what extent does this description actually apply to Sir Toby? What is your view of Sir Toby at this point in the play?

Act 4

4.1 Summary: *Feste talks to Sebastian, thinking he is Cesario; Sir Andrew, Sir Toby and Fabian make the same error, leading to a fight between Sebastian and Sir Andrew; Feste fetches Olivia, who restores order and invites Sebastian back to her house.*

Act 4 intensifies the confusion from the previous scene, as Sebastian enters the world of the other characters for the first time. Feste declares that 'nothing that is so is so' (l.6–7) – a statement that makes no sense yet sums up the characters' circumstances perfectly. Sebastian, too, is baffled by the chaotic situation he has walked into, as he is attacked apparently for no reason: 'Are all the people mad?' (l.23).

However, Olivia settles the simmering tensions and imposes her authority, which has been largely absent with Sir Toby creating mayhem. Now, finally, she calls him out:

> Ungracious wretch,
> Fit for the mountains and the barbarous caves,
> Where manner ne'er were preached! (l.40–2)

Sir Toby has a little more mischief to do (in the next scene), but his time of misrule is running out.

Sebastian ends the scene as bewildered as he begins it, but happily so – he concludes that he is either mad or dreaming, but is content to submit to Olivia's command. The 'madness' of love in the play now finds its first happy ending; other kinds of madness, though, are yet to be resolved.

4.2 Summary: *Malvolio is put in a dark room and visited by Feste, Sir Toby and Maria; Feste pretends to be Sir Topas, a curate; they treat Malvolio as if he is genuinely mad; he writes a letter to Olivia.*

The question of madness is central to this scene, and Malvolio, despite Sir Toby, Maria and Feste attempting to convince him otherwise, insists plausibly on his sanity. The idea of madness is explored using imagery of darkness:

> They have here propertied me: keep me in darkness, send ministers to me, asses, and do all they can to face me out of my wits. (l.77–9)

Although he appears to believe that Sir Topas really is a man of religion, not Feste in disguise, Malvolio shows his complete understanding of what has been done to him, and his insistence that he is 'no more mad than you are' (l.38) and that he has been 'notoriously abused' (l.73, a phrase echoed by Olivia at 5.1.356) rings true.

Sir Toby now begins to find Malvolio's distress less amusing, since he is 'in offence with [his] niece' and 'cannot pursue with any safety this sport' (l.56–7). Characteristically, it is his own 'safety' he thinks of, not the safety of others.

Key point

Malvolio uses darkness in a metaphorical as well as a literal sense when he says 'this house is as dark as ignorance' (l.36), calling out the true nature of Sir Toby and Maria's cruel, mocking behaviour. Darkness, madness, disorder and confusion have characterised events in Olivia's household, but they are soon to be replaced by clarity and order.

Q Feste plays a stronger part than previously in the deception of Malvolio, pretending to be a curate and trying to convince Malvolio that he is truly mad. Does this make Feste a less sympathetic character? Why or why not?

4.3 Summary: *Sebastian agrees to exchange vows with Olivia, although he is still confused by what has happened.*

This short scene establishes the loving connection between Sebastian and Olivia, which in turn is the basis for both Olivia and Orsino becoming angry with Viola in the final scene. In a soliloquy, Sebastian continues the play's exploration of madness, though he also considers whether 'this may be some error' (l.10) – which of course it is – or whether it is a form of 'wonder' that 'enwraps' him (l.3). The word 'wonder' is echoed in the next scene by Olivia's 'most wonderful' (5.1.209), and from this point most of the various forms of 'madness' will be resolved and transformed into happiness and wonder.

Sebastian's comment on Olivia's ability to run her household provides a rare insight into her proficiency. Previously, when she was concerned for Malvolio's welfare, she asked, 'Where's my cousin Toby?'

(3.4.55), betraying her ignorance of Sir Toby's schemes as well as her reluctance to impose herself. Now, though, Sebastian testifies to her ability to run her large household efficiently and calmly, acknowledging the way she can 'command her followers, / Take and give back affairs' with a 'smooth, discreet and stable bearing' (l.17–19). These qualities are also evident in Olivia's calm and considered reactions to the many confusions in the play's concluding act.

Q What does Sebastian mean when he says, 'I am ready to distrust mine eyes, / And wrangle with my reason that persuades me' (l.13–14)?

Act 5

5.1 Summary: *Orsino and Viola arrive at Olivia's property; the officers bring Antonio, who continues to insist that 'Cesario' is Sebastian. Orsino is angry when Olivia addresses Cesario as 'husband' (l.132); Viola protests, but is interrupted by the arrival of Sir Andrew and Sir Toby, bleeding from a fight. Sebastian enters, accepting responsibility for their injuries; everyone is bewildered by how similar Sebastian and Cesario appear, and each twin takes time to accept that their sibling is alive. Viola reveals her true identity, leading Orsino to offer his hand in marriage; Olivia hears Malvolio's letter read out by Fabian and also sees Maria's, and realises that Malvolio has been tricked and abused.*

The single long scene in Act 5 draws together the play's narrative threads, resolving most of the tensions and conflicts and ending with the prospect of imminent marriages between Olivia and Sebastian, as well as Viola and Orsino – a double-marriage ending typical of Shakespeare's comedies.

A series of misunderstandings escalates tensions before all the threads can be untangled. Antonio thinks Cesario is Sebastian; Olivia believes Viola to be the same person she has recently exchanged vows with, and thus calls her 'husband' (l.132). Viola is baffled, but Orsino, feeling deeply betrayed, is furious. He calls Viola a 'dissembling cub' (l.153) and tells her to go 'where thou and I henceforth may never meet' (l.158). The tension is briefly relieved by the comical entrances of the injured Sir Andrew and Sir Toby; Sebastian has defeated them in a swordfight, and they now appear pathetic and powerless. In Act 1 Sir Toby praised Sir Andrew (if only facetiously) for having 'all the good gifts of nature' (1.3.23), but now he contemptuously calls him 'an ass-head, and a coxcomb, and a knave' (l.190), exposing his true opinion.

Sebastian's entry brings about yet another shift in tone. The pathos of his reunion with Viola is heightened by the others' astonishment as well as by the twins' own restrained responses. They mistrust appearances, instead seeking out the underlying reality, proving their identities by exchanging details of their lives that only they could know. Viola defers their 'embrace' (l.235) until she can truly confirm her identity by reclaiming her 'maiden weeds' (l.239), thus matching her outward appearance to her inner sense of self.

Near the end, Feste declares that 'the whirligig of time brings in his revenges' (l.353–4), suggesting that time has indeed resolved conflicts and 'untie[d]' the 'knot' (2.2.38). But Feste is thinking only of Malvolio being punished for calling him 'a barren rascal' (l.353); the cruel treatment of Malvolio by 'Sir Toby, and the lighter people' (l.318) is in fact well in excess of any wrong he has done to others. While the misunderstandings surrounding Viola's disguise have been resolved by Sebastian's appearance, and Sir Toby's influence has ended, Malvolio's threat to 'be revenged' (l.355) lingers.

Feste's final song also contributes a dark note at the end of this comedy, with the haunting phrases 'the wind and the rain' (l.367) and 'the rain it raineth every day' (l.369) pointing to life's struggles and deprivations. Against that, however, is the joy of theatre and the actors' promise to 'strive to please you every day' (l.385).

Q Antonio and Orsino both indicate that it has been three months since the events at the start of the play. Does this come as a surprise? Why or why not?

Q The full title of the play is *Twelfth Night, or What You Will*. How does the second part of the title relate to the play's events?

CHARACTERS & RELATIONSHIPS

Viola

Key quotes

'Not yet old enough for a man, nor young enough for a boy … He is very well-favoured and he speaks very shrewishly.' (Malvolio, 1.5.130–3)

'… I swear, I am not that I play.' (1.5.153)

'A lady, sir, though it was said she much resembled me, was yet of many accounted beautiful … she bore a mind that envy could not but call fair.' (Sebastian of Viola, 2.1.18–21)

While Malvolio and Orsino remark on Cesario's youth, the play does not specify the age of Viola and her twin Sebastian (or indeed of the other characters). Most commentators speculate that at least some years have passed since the death of their father when they were thirteen; Viola is commonly played by actors in their twenties.

Despite beginning the play in grief and distress – having just survived a traumatic shipwreck that she believes claimed the life of her dear twin brother – Viola is resilient and resourceful, immediately devising ways to survive her new environment. Many scholars consider her passive in comparison to other Shakespearean comic heroines; for example, Elizabeth Schafer says 'Viola can be a problematic heroine. She expects fate to sort things out for her' (Schafer 1995, p.229). However, Viola shows more agency than several other characters (e.g. Sebastian, Antonio, Malvolio or even Orsino): managing her own affairs, thinking on her feet when delivering Orsino's messages, and holding her own intellectually in word play with Feste. Her very first line is a question, indicating her curiosity and engagement with the world around her.

Viola is loyal and trustworthy – serving her master Orsino even when Olivia makes it difficult – and kind, willingly sharing half her money with Antonio, a stranger, despite her limited funds ('lean and low ability',

3.4.294–5). She is also good-natured and avoids upsetting others: when confronted by Sir Toby about Sir Andrew's grievance, she confidently declares, 'I am sure no man hath any quarrel to me. My remembrance is very free and clear from any image of offence done to any man' (3.4.192–4). Similarly, her assertions 'I am no fighter' (3.4.206) and 'I am one that had rather go with sir priest than sir knight' (3.4.229–30) reflect not just her hidden identity as a woman (therefore untrained in duelling) but her peaceable nature.

Integrity: Viola as Cesario

Although Viola is performing a role for most of the play, there is no indication that we see anything other than her true personality. In disguise, she is obligated and restricted in certain ways: she must do as her employer wishes (and must keep secret her love for him), and is unable to tell Olivia why the lady should not develop an affection for her. But in all other ways Cesario *is* Viola: in her brief appearances as Viola rather than Cesario, there are no significant differences in the way she speaks, thinks or acts.

While her performance of two simultaneous selves might seem evidence of duplicitousness, her disguise is not for malicious reasons – rather, it is for practicality and protection. Nor does she use her disguise to gain knowledge or influence, even when that might be to her advantage. Despite falling in love with Orsino, she is steadfast in trying to make his case to Olivia.

Olivia

Key quotes

'O when mine eyes did see Olivia first,
Methought she purged the air of pestilence …' (Orsino, 1.1.19–20)

'A virtuous maid, the daughter of a count
That died some twelvemonth since, then leaving her
In the protection of his son, her brother,

Who shortly also died; for whose dear love
(They say) she hath abjured the sight
And company of men.' (Captain, 1.2.36–41)

'... being addicted to a melancholy as she is ...' (Maria, 2.5.168)

Following the deaths of her father and brother, Olivia is in charge of her court (a situation possibly modelled on the young Queen Elizabeth I coming to the throne, decades before *Twelfth Night*'s first performance). Her financial independence gives her social status, and Orsino's adoration and Malvolio's yearning establish her as an unattainable object of desire, adding emotional status. Although her uncle might be expected to hold some sway, he is clearly less responsible and less respectable than Olivia, and she is never under his guardianship.

Olivia is emotionally volatile. She begins the play in a state of mourning, refusing the company of men, with no interest in Orsino's affections. But on meeting Cesario she becomes animated and falls swiftly in love, committing to pursuing him, despite realising the inappropriateness of the match. However, Sir Toby claims 'she'll not match above her degree, neither in estate [or] years' (1.3.89–90), so perhaps part of what attracts her to Cesario is his lesser status.

Key point

Interestingly, Olivia falls in love with someone (Cesario) who does not desperately desire her (as Orsino and Malvolio do).

Olivia is generally compassionate with her staff and attendants. For instance, she tries to ensure Malvolio is treated well after discovering 'he hath been most notoriously abused' (5.1.356): 'Let some of my people have a special care of him; I would not have him miscarry for the half of my dowry' (3.4.56–7). She also engages in word play with Feste and is sometimes lenient with him: although he is 'dishonest' in visiting Orsino's household (1.5.34), he is certainly not 'hanged' for it as Maria threatens he might be (1.5.14).

Orsino

Key quotes

'... I suppose him virtuous, know him noble,
Of great estate, of fresh and stainless youth;
In voices well divulged, free, learned, and valiant,
And in dimension, and the shape of nature,
A gracious person.' (Olivia, 1.5.213–17)

'... such as I am, all true lovers are,
Unstaid and skittish in all motions else,
Save in the constant image of the creature
That is beloved.' (2.4.15–18)

Orsino opens the play, with his famous 'If music be the food of love' speech, but subsequently appears in only three scenes, with fewer lines than any other main character. Apart from in the opening scene, he is always with Cesario, somewhat isolated from the rest of the plot; even his deep connection with Olivia is at a physical distance.

Often speaking in poetic monologues rich with descriptive language, hyperbole and figurative devices such as metaphor, Orsino can be self-aggrandising, such as when he claims, 'There is no woman's sides / Can bide the beating of so strong a passion / As love doth give my heart' (2.4.89–91), and considers his love 'more noble than the world' (2.4.77).

Out of desperation in his unrequited love for Olivia, Orsino sends Cesario as a messenger – which sets in motion the Olivia/Cesario subplot – but ultimately he seems to transfer that devotion easily to Viola, with whom (as Cesario) he has bonded quickly and deeply. As Valentine observes to Cesario, Orsino 'hath known you but three days, and already you are no stranger' (1.4.2–3) and 'like to be much advanced' (1.4.2) – a foreshadowing of what's to come, when Viola is married to Orsino.

Like the more comic characters, Orsino does not grow or change much throughout the play. His defining feature is a deep passion, for which he finally finds a receptive vessel in Viola.

Maria

Key quotes

'... you must confine yourself within the modest limits of order.' (1.3.6–7)

'... I know my physic will work with him.' (2.3.145–6)

Sir Andrew: ... she's a good wench.
Sir Toby: She's a beagle, true bred, and one that adores me. (2.3.150–1)

Maria is one of Olivia's attendants: Sir Toby calls her a 'chambermaid' (1.3.42) but some critics emphasise her status as 'a companion ... not a servant' (Schafer 1995, p.231). With Sir Toby and Sir Andrew, she makes up the trio of 'tricksters' (a useful grouping for analysis, though the term belies the extent of the trio's cruelty), which Feste and Fabian also join.

Confident and playful, Maria sustains verbal parrying with Sir Toby and Sir Andrew (e.g. first half of Act 1, Scene 3) and with Feste (beginning of Act 1, Scene 5). She is also conniving, devising and executing the plan to trap Malvolio with the letter (and further punish him through Sir Topas) apparently 'for the love of mockery' (2.5.15), but her creativity has its roots in unkindness. Here, perhaps, lies her main connection with Sir Toby: both have a malicious streak, taking joy in others' suffering. (Besides this, there is little explanation of why they marry, as Maria never expresses affection for Sir Toby. Rather, she seems to find his drunken foolery tedious, saying he must 'come in earlier o'nights', 1.3.3.) The trick, concocted to exact 'revenge' for Malvolio's perceived character faults (2.3.129), is implemented with no concern for his feelings or his humanity. Maria is also abrasive with Malvolio, dismissing him rudely despite his senior position within Olivia's household: 'Go shake your ears' (2.3.106) effectively labels him an ass.

Feste

Key quotes

'There is no slander in an allowed fool …' (Olivia, 1.5.76)

'Come away, come away, death,
And in sad cypress let me be laid.' (2.4.49–50)

'This fellow is wise enough to play the fool,
And to do that well craves a kind of wit …' (Viola, 3.1.50–1)

Feste, a professional ('allowed') fool in Olivia's court, is an example of a 'wise fool', as distinct from the derogatory 'natural fool' (an ignorant person, e.g. Maria calls Sir Andrew a 'fool', 1.3.24). Professional fools or jesters were employed in Elizabethan households to entertain royalty or nobility, their position sometimes giving them freedom to say things not otherwise acceptable. For example, Feste makes fun of Olivia (in the 'take away the fool' interchange, 1.5.32–59). Olivia engages Feste in witty banter, but chides him for 'old' (stale) humour (1.5.91) and for his absence when he is at Orsino's court. When Feste reads Malvolio's letter aloud, she tires of his demonstrative foolery and snatches it away to be read by Fabian instead (5.1.281).

Although he has scenes with all key characters, traversing both noble houses and both groups of characters (the 'lovers' and 'tricksters'), Feste is at a remove from the action. Little he does affords insight into his character; all is part of his professional 'performance' (as we are reminded when he is paid by or requests money from characters, including Orsino and both twins). In becoming Sir Topas he adds an extra layer of performativity, even donning a costume (despite Malvolio being unable to see him, 4.2.51–2).

Key point

Shakespeare's company contained notable professional 'clowns' for whom he wrote his 'fool' roles (including Feste in *Twelfth Night* and the Fool in *King Lear*). Scholars agree that Feste was written for Robert Armin, who was musically talented, which explains why Feste has so many songs.

Unlike other Shakespearean fools, Feste contributes to the plot's progression. Like Sir Toby and Maria, he is disturbingly cruel to Malvolio; he 'gaslights' him as Sir Topas, telling him the dark, locked room is full of light, and asking questions only to twist his answers to prove him mad.

Feste's role is ostensibly comic: many of his scenes involve wit, in mutual verbal 'sparring' matches following formalised rhetorical structures (as when he must 'catechise' Olivia to 'prove' she is the fool, 1.5.51 and 47). Yet he carries an air of melancholy – many of his songs are bleak in tone – and some productions interpret him as bringing a darker element to the play.

Sir Toby Belch

Key quotes

'I'll confine myself no finer than I am: these clothes are good enough to drink in, and so be these boots too …' (1.3.8–9)

'Dost thou think because thou art virtuous there shall be no more cakes and ale?' (to Malvolio, 2.3.97–9)

'… I am now so far in offence with my niece that I cannot pursue with any safety this sport to the upshot.' (4.2.55–7)

Sir Toby, Olivia's uncle (they sometimes refer to each other as 'cousin', a general term for a relation), is a friend of Sir Andrew and is fond of Maria, whom he eventually marries. He is a guest at Olivia's house although she tells him, via Malvolio, that she is unimpressed with his drunkenness and that, if it continues, she would be 'very willing to bid [him] farewell' (2.3.85).

Frivolous, tipsy, bawdy and slightly absurd, Sir Toby is dismissive of any expectations of respectable, considerate behaviour. Maria reports Olivia has said 'quaffing and drinking will undo you' (1.3.11), but he is never chastened by repeated requests to moderate his noise and his drinking. This insight into his attitude contextualises the insensitivity of the tricks played against both Malvolio and Sir Toby's own supposed friend Sir Andrew.

Sir Toby is often drunk, as is indicated by his frequent misuse of words ('substractors' for detractors, 1.3.28; his confusion of Olivia's 'lethargy' with 'lechery', 1.5.102–3). In performance, his intoxication is usually played for comedy, with the kind of slapstick suggested by stage directions: in his second scene, he is *'staggering'* (stage direction preceding 1.5.95) and *'hiccuping'* (1.5.99), and in his third scene he calls for more wine (2.3.12), singing and carousing. Yet when Feste claims the surgeon is drunk, Sir Toby exclaims, 'I hate a drunken rogue' (5.1.185–6). While this is humorous irony, it also shows unkindness: Sir Toby does not admit his own failings but is quick to judge them in others.

Although Sir Toby has the most lines in the play, he does not appear to develop as a character, or to experience (let alone learn from) significant consequences of his actions. His behaviour towards Malvolio and Sir Andrew is never punished (except inadvertently, perhaps, by Sebastian injuring him). On the contrary, he is somewhat arbitrarily rewarded with marriage, leaving him with a 'happy ending' denied to characters such as Malvolio and Antonio.

Sir Andrew Aguecheek

Key quotes

'... I think [life] ... consists of eating and drinking.' (2.3.9–10)

'For Andrew, if he were opened and you find so much blood in his liver as will clog the foot of a flea, I'll eat the rest of th'anatomy.' (Sir Toby, 3.2.48–9)

Sir Andrew is a pitiful character who is easily manipulated by his 'friend' Sir Toby, and participates heartily, if passively, in rowdy drunkenness and tricking Malvolio. Like Sir Toby, Sir Andrew does not appear to grow or learn from his actions, ending the play with less than he began with (since he gives Cesario his horse, and Sir Toby's frivolity costs him thousands of ducats). Unsurprisingly, any attempts to commend him as a worthy suitor for Olivia are undermined by evidence to the contrary.

- 'He's as tall a man as any's in Illyria' (Sir Toby, 1.3.16; 'tall' here meaning 'brave'), but Sir Andrew's cowardice in the duel disproves this.
- Sir Toby declares Sir Andrew 'has three thousand ducats a year' (1.3.18), but Maria notes he will foolishly waste it all.
- Sir Toby says Sir Andrew has musical and linguistic talents, but Sir Andrew fails to understand simple French (1.3.77).

Sir Andrew is often a figure of justified ridicule. In his first scene he flails, attempting to keep up with Sir Toby and Maria's jesting and word play. In Act 2, Scene 3, when planning the trick against Malvolio, Maria and Sir Toby again dominate, and Sir Andrew's lines are generally short, inconsequential interjections. Later, when the tricksters watch Malvolio decipher the letter, Sir Andrew fails to understand jokes, making a series of weak comments such as 'so could I, too' (2.5.151, and similarly 153, 156, 159, 171), tagging onto Sir Toby's lines. He gormlessly does whatever Sir Toby tells him to, whether courting Olivia, staying longer at the house, funding the drinking sessions or fighting Cesario.

One positive trait is Sir Andrew's lack of vanity: while he praises his own dancing abilities ('I think I have the back-trick simply as strong as any man in Illyria', 1.3.100–1), he is happy to admit he has 'no more wit than … an ordinary man' (1.3.70–1) and is aware of his reputation as 'a foolish knight' (2.5.63–4). He also appears trustworthy: after promising Cesario his horse, he says 'for that I promised you, I'll be as good as my word' (3.4.274–5).

Malvolio

Key quotes

'O you are sick of self-love, Malvolio, and taste with a distempered appetite.' (Olivia, 1.5.73–4)

'... sometimes he is a kind of puritan.' (Maria, 2.3.119)

'... I say there was never man thus abused. I am no more mad than you are.' (4.2.37–8)

Malvolio is Olivia's steward. Stewards were senior servants in charge of a noble's estate, and their responsibilities included managing the property, finances and other household servants. Such duties contextualise his attitude towards Maria, Sir Toby and Sir Andrew: Malvolio is not merely a stuffy killjoy; rather, their drunkenness and poor behaviour reflect directly on the household he oversees. This might encourage us to empathise with him, and to judge harshly those characters who cruelly trick him.

However, Shakespeare gives Malvolio unpleasant characteristics – smugness, intolerance, overambitiousness, self-importance – limiting our sympathy for him (at least until the 'prank' goes too far). Malvolio also embodies the religious and political Puritanism that was increasing in strength in Elizabethan England, and was seen by some as extremist. Shakespeare could have expected many of his audience to join him and the other characters in objecting to what Malvolio stood for (and therefore in being amused by the tricksters' treatment of him).

Malvolio harbours an inappropriate aspiration 'to be Count Malvolio!' (2.5.30) and has such confidence in his own worth that it takes little (the false letter) for him to see himself stepping into that role. His desire for Olivia does not seem to be genuine love, as he expresses no specific fondness for her – unlike affections expressed by, for example, Orsino for Olivia, Viola for Orsino, or Olivia for Cesario. Rather, his fantasies are associated with power and position: he imagines 'sitting in my state' (2.5.38), and dreams of luxury, ordering his staff about, lecturing Sir Toby about his drunkenness and criticising Sir Andrew.

Sebastian

Key quotes

'... my father was that Sebastian of Messaline ... He left behind him myself and a sister, both born in an hour: if the heavens had been pleased, would we had so ended!' (2.1.12–15)

'... my bosom is full of kindness, and I am yet so near the manners of my mother that, upon the least occasion more, mine eyes will tell tales of me.' (2.1.28–31)

We learn less about Sebastian than about his twin, Viola, and his role in the story is much smaller. He only has around thirty speeches (compared to Viola's over eighty), and we do not meet him until Act 2. However, he is significant for how he inspires Viola in her enactment of Cesario. In some ways Sebastian is also a foil for Viola, with their physical similarity underscoring behavioural differences, in that he has little apparent sense of purpose on arriving in Illyria, deciding simply to 'go see the relics of this town' (3.3.19) and relying on Antonio's assistance, whereas Viola immediately devises a plan to sustain herself. Even in love he seems passive (if hasty!): he agrees to go with Olivia seconds after meeting her. However, he does appear loyal, promising Olivia he 'ever will be true' (4.3.33).

Initially Sebastian resists Antonio's offers of support, compassionately worrying 'the malignancy of my fate might perhaps distemper yours' (2.1.2–3), and insisting the only thing Antonio could do for him would be to undo saving his life (since Sebastian thinks Viola did not survive, and therefore he has little will to live). However, he soon seems dependent on Antonio's support.

In Act 4, when repeatedly mistaken for Cesario, Sebastian's confusion indicates that it doesn't occur to him that Viola is alive. He believes everyone around him mad, and his response to Sir Andrew's challenge is to physically lash out in defence (4.1.22), illustrating a clichéd masculine behaviour that contrasts with Viola's long poetic conversations with Orsino and Olivia, and her strong reluctance to fight.

Antonio

Key quote

'I could not stay behind you. My desire,
More sharp than filèd steel, did spur me forth …' (3.3.4–5)

Antonio, a sea captain who helped Sebastian survive the shipwreck, is described in the cast list as a 'friend' to Sebastian (although in Act 2, Scene 1, Sebastian explains his history to Antonio, suggesting that they did not know each other before the shipwreck). Antonio's actions and words – including 'love', 'adore' and 'desire' – suggest his affections for Sebastian are deeper than simple friendship. Though Shakespeare did not have the freedom to explicitly portray same-sex love, the intensity of Antonio's feelings leads many modern interpretations to present his character this way.

Whether or not his feelings for Sebastian are romantic, Antonio's devotion is unflagging. Even when apprehended by Illyrian officers he is less upset by the arrest than by the fact it means he can no longer be with Sebastian: 'it grieves me / Much more for what I cannot do for you / Than what befalls myself' (3.4.285–7).

Minor characters

The **Captain** who helps Viola settle into Illyria was 'bred and born / Not three hours' travel' from where they land (1.2.22–3) so is able to provide exposition that helps orient Viola (and therefore the audience). **Valentine** and **Curio**, attendants to Orsino, appear briefly in several scenes. **Fabian**, one of Olivia's servants, has a comparatively larger role, with lines in key scenes such as Malvolio's letter-reading (2.5); he tells Olivia 'myself and Toby' came up with the prank (5.1.338), graciously leaving Maria relatively blame-free. The **Priest** who marries Olivia and Cesario is an actual holy priest, not to be confused with **Sir Topas** the pretend curate (clergyman), who is Feste in disguise.

THEMES, IDEAS & VALUES

Love

Key quotes

'O spirit of love, how quick and fresh art thou ...' (Orsino, 1.1.9)

'But come what may, I do adore thee so
That danger shall seem sport, and I will go.' (Antonio about Sebastian, 2.1.35–6)

'Love sought is good, but giv'n unsought is better.' (Olivia, 3.1.141)

The word 'love' appears around a hundred times in *Twelfth Night,* which explores familial love (the twins' affections for one another; Olivia's dedication to mourning her brother and father), same-sex love (in the 'mistaken' pairings between Olivia and Viola, or Orsino and Cesario; also in Antonio's care for Sebastian, depending on interpretation), platonic love (Antonio's for Sebastian, in some interpretations) and 'self love' (Malvolio's). Even secondary plots, such as the gulling of Malvolio and Sir Andrew, revolve around love: the goal of the trick against Malvolio is to make him believe Olivia loves him, and the ostensible reason for Sir Andrew fighting Cesario is to compete for Olivia's affection.

The main form of love represented is romantic love, particularly in the central Orsino–Viola–Olivia triangle. Romantic love is portrayed as:

- all-consuming and often uncontrollable: 'My love can give no place, bide no denay' (Orsino, 2.4.120)
- analogous to an illness: 'Even so quickly may one catch the plague?' (Olivia, 1.5.250)
- poetic (as in Viola's 'willow cabin' speech, 1.5.223–31).

While these three lovers have 'happily ever after' endings, the outcomes for each are not as they had imagined, suggesting there may be an arbitrariness to fate, or a predetermined plan not discernible by participants. Orsino will marry Viola rather than Olivia; Olivia ends up with Sebastian instead of Cesario. In further evidence for the randomness of love, Antonio – constant and loyal – ends up alone, while Sir Toby and Maria, who are both unkind to others, are 'rewarded' with marriage to each other, despite little evidence of affection between them. Although Sir Toby claims Maria 'adores' him (2.3.151), she never demonstrates this fondness in her words or actions.

The play's focus on various forms of love suggests that – at least in the quasi-carnivalesque atmosphere of misrule and festivity that is Twelfth Night – love is the essence of life. However, the speed with which many characters fall in love and marry, and the fact that many change the targets of their affection equally quickly, also suggests that love may be trivial or superficial: 'at once capacious and enveloping, love is at the same time ephemeral and destined to disappointment' (Charles 1997, p.139).

Gendered love

Although it is difficult to untangle the representations of gendered experiences of love in this play (particularly due to the protagonist's three layers of gender: male actor / female character / male disguise), various characters attempt to differentiate the qualities of male and female love:

- 'We men may say more, swear more, but indeed / Our shows are more than will: for still we prove / Much in our vows, but little in our love' (Viola, 2.4.112–14)
- 'Our fancies are more giddy and unfirm, / More longing, wavering, sooner lost and worn, / Than women's are' (Orsino, 2.4.31–3).

Orsino contradicts the above statement, however, insisting that Cesario 'make no compare / Between that love a woman can bear me, / And that I owe Olivia' (2.4.97–9). To some extent his high opinion of the intensity of his own love sets him up for failure: what chance has he of happiness if he believes his love will always be greater than any woman's could be? Perhaps this is a hint that it is 'Cesario' – not exactly a woman to Orsino, even at the end of the play when all is revealed, since she remains in male clothes and he still calls her 'boy' (5.1.251) – who will be able to satisfy him.

Or perhaps Orsino's experience suggests love is more about passion itself than the object of it. Though he claims the one thing men are 'constant' about in life is the object of their love (2.4.17), he disproves this when he lightly exchanges Olivia for Viola (via a preoccupation with Cesario, suggesting that even gender is less important than love itself). As the director of the 2023 Bell Shakespeare production noted, love in Elizabethan productions 'transcended gender and sexuality, instead emphasising the human need for connection while acknowledging the multiplicity of romantic identities' (Fairbairn 2023).

Constancy

Antonio is the play's case study in constancy. He saves Sebastian's life: although the Captain tells Viola in Act 1, Scene 2 that he saw Sebastian tie *himself* to a mast, Sebastian says Antonio 'took [him] from the breach of the sea' (2.1.15–16) and 'recovered' him (2.1.28). Antonio begs Sebastian to let him be his 'servant' (2.1.26); while Sebastian declines, it is clear when we next see them (Act 3, Scene 3) that Antonio has insisted on accompanying him, despite his history in Illyria making this risky. Later, he gives Sebastian money ('here's my purse', 3.4.38), not just for lodgings but to spoil himself, in case he should see any 'toy' he fancies (3.3.44).

Antonio also steps in unhesitatingly when he thinks he sees Sebastian about to duel with Sir Andrew, offering to sacrifice himself instead: 'If this young gentleman / Have done offence, I take the fault on me; / If you offend him, I for him defy you' (3.4.264–6).

Faithfulness in love is something both Orsino and Olivia claim to have but fail to display. Antonio, conversely, remains devoted to Sebastian, through trials and, as far as we know, even beyond the play – since the conclusion leaves Antonio's fate unaddressed. We know only that his loyalty is not rewarded, and Sebastian marries Olivia. This is further evidence for the argument that love can be cruel and fickle.

Sex, gender and sexuality

Key quotes

'... thy small pipe
Is as the maiden's organ, shrill and sound,
And all is semblative a woman's part.' (Orsino to Cesario, 1.4.31–3)

'... As I am man,
My state is desperate for my master's love;
As I am woman – now alas the day! –
What thriftless sighs shall poor Olivia breathe?' (Viola, 2.2.33–6)

'A little thing would make me tell them how much I lack of a man.' (Viola, 3.4.255–6)

Twelfth Night poses many questions that it leaves unanswered, including:

- how sex, gender and sexuality are linked (particularly, whether sex and gender dictate love)
- how gender is constructed (this may seem a more modern question, but Viola's gendered 'disguise', and other characters' responses, is an interrogation of the difference between biological sex and gender expression)
- whether gender can be determined by external experience.

While the themes of gender and sex are as central to the play as love, they are represented differently: love is mentioned constantly, while notions of gender are presented implicitly – through events, characters and relationships. Although there are explicit discussions of Cesario's physical appearance (specifically his resemblance to a woman), and Viola frequently makes thinly veiled comments about her true nature, the explorations of gender exist in the interpretive space between text and audience, underscored in the cross-dressing of the protagonist.

This cross-dressing (and resultant confusions of love) generates so many complicated, overlapping dimensions of gender relations that it is impossible to read the play as arguing anything other than that sex, gender and sexuality are, at their most conservative, complex; and, at their most radical, fluid. For example, the Olivia–Viola/Cesario dynamic can be read by audiences (depending on directorial, casting and acting decisions) as representing:

- same-sex attraction/frisson between women (Viola and Olivia)
- same-sex attraction between men (the actors playing Olivia and Viola on an Elizabethan stage or in modern all-male casts)
- heterosexual attraction between a male and a female (Cesario and Olivia).

The last is, in a way, the most complex, since much is made of how feminine 'Cesario' is: if Olivia is falling for a man, as the script asserts, it is for an unconventionally feminine one.

Similarly, the Orsino–Cesario/Viola dynamic can be read as existing between two males (Orsino and Cesario; also the two male actors) or between a male and a female (Orsino and Viola). Any one of these multiple readings are encouraged, at any given moment, by what is taking place in the scene, and the audience, unlike the characters, always shares Viola's 'secret', understanding the dramatic irony of her situation. For Shakespearean audiences, this was a doubly-disguised identity, and in modern interpretations – even if the performance features a female actor as Viola – we are haunted by the shadow of the boy-actor and the additional level of gender disguise.

Key point

Although Viola is the focal point for notions of gender, other characters also contribute to this theme. For example, Sir Toby, teasing Malvolio, addresses him within a single speech as both 'bawcock' and 'chuck' (3.4.98) – the former traditionally a masculine term of endearment, and the latter traditionally female. Even when the scene is not explicitly addressing gender, language emphasises the fluidity of seemingly fixed categories.

The plot device of identical twins of different gender (which is of course biologically impossible, requiring the audience to suspend disbelief) allows Shakespeare to explore sex and gender as two 'halves' of a whole. Sebastian and Viola are presented as a single entity: the actions of one impact on the other, and until the final scene the characters around them believe them to be one person. This duality is echoed in Viola's double-gendered body. Olivia believes she has exchanged vows with Cesario and is ultimately happy to be marrying Sebastian, even though she fell in love with the wit and character of Viola, emphasising the fluidity of gender and reinforcing the idea that romantic love may be more about the experience of being in love than the object of affection. Similarly, Orsino's language choices in the final scene – he continues to call Viola 'Cesario' and 'boy' (5.1.251), and says 'you are a man' who will, in 'other habits', become 'Orsino's mistress' (5.1.363–5) – allude to a view of sex and gender that is not fixed but responsive to situation and interpretation.

Identity, performance and disguise

Key quotes

'Conceal me what I am ...
For such disguise as haply shall become
The form of my intent.' (Viola, 1.2.53–5)

'... I am not that I play.' (Viola, 1.5.153)

'Fortune forbid my outside have not charmed her!' (Viola, 2.2.15)

Like gender, identity in *Twelfth Night* is shown to be malleable and sometimes diverse – even within individuals. Viola's disguise as Cesario (and her 'performance' of the Duke's lines she delivers to Olivia) is central to this, but the idea of constructed identities is not limited to one character. Feste also embodies the notion of performance, as he is always playing a role – mainly as Olivia's fool but also notably in Act 4, Scene 2 as Sir Topas. He also proposes to perform the role of 'madness' when reading Malvolio's letter in Act 5, Scene 1. Maria, similarly, 'performs' the role of Olivia in writing the fake letter. Even Sebastian chooses for some reason to temporarily hide his true identity, going by 'Roderigo' (2.1.12).

Olivia, when she first meets Cesario, hides behind a veil. Productions often have Maria and sometimes other household staff covered by veils here, to hide Olivia's identity even further. At first Olivia refuses to identify herself as the lady of the house but says she will 'answer for her' (1.5.140), maintaining mystery – perhaps for her own amusement, perhaps to avoid Orsino's unwelcome courting.

All these examples show that, when it facilitates an end goal, people may construct identities, presenting themselves as other than they are.

Key point

Disguise allows characters to voice things they might not otherwise be able to say, such as Viola criticising men's inconstancy in love: 'We men may say more, swear more, but indeed ... prove ... little in our love' (2.4.112–14). Similarly, Feste's motley (fool's clothing) allows him to get away with expressing things he otherwise could not.

There are also points where Shakespeare provides 'in-jokes' for the audience through his characters – when their lines show an awareness of the play as performance. Examples include:

- Viola's 'I am not that I play' (1.5.153)
- Fabian's 'if this were played upon a stage now, I could condemn it as an improbable fiction' (3.4.108–9)
- Sir Andrew's 'I would not undertake her in this company' (1.3.48, with 'this company' referring to the audience).

The characters are not breaking the fourth wall, as these lines are directed not at the audience but at characters in the scene, but such moments indicate the playwright's preoccupation with the notions of disguise, performance and constructed identity. *Twelfth Night* thus acknowledges the illusions of theatre, drawing parallels with the illusions characters create within the world of the play.

Madness

Key quotes

'... he speaks nothing but madman. Fie on him.' (Olivia about Sir Toby, 1.5.87–8)

'I am no more mad than you are.' (Malvolio to 'Sir Topas', 4.2.38)

'Or I am mad, or else this is a dream.' (Sebastian, 4.1.54)

'... he does nothing but smile ... for sure the man is tainted in's wits.' (Maria, 3.4.11–13)

The theme of madness links the multiple plots. For Orsino and Olivia (and to some extent Viola) love is a kind of madness, while the tricksters attempt to gull Malvolio into losing his sanity: 'we shall make him mad indeed' (3.4.112). The broader setting of the play – the misrule of Twelfth Night – also represents a kind of sanctioned madness: people behaving wildly and irrationally in ways society wouldn't tolerate at other times.

Madness in the play is conceived as not being in one's right mind, and is always depicted as a negative state. Despite the play's festival setting, links between playful 'foolery' and madness, and Olivia's description of Malvolio's behaviour as innocuous 'midsummer madness' (3.4.50), a loss of rational function is associated with the darker aspects of the play – most particularly the attempted gaslighting of Malvolio. The Sir Topas scene (4.2) is unsettling, showing individuals maliciously weaponising the fragility of mental equilibrium.

Madness is also seen as an imbalance or contradiction between feelings and understanding; as Sebastian puts it when trying to fathom the dreamlike events around him, 'my soul disputes well with my sense' (4.3.9). This could also describe the lovers' experiences, particularly that of Olivia, who opens the play vowing to renounce 'the sight / And company of men' (1.2.40–1) but quickly falls in love with Cesario almost against her will: her soul and sense are in discord. Orsino, similarly, can be seen to succumb to a mad affection when he is drawn to Cesario: ultimately his sense and soul are united in a kind of sanity when Cesario is revealed as Viola and they are free to marry.

Another conceptualisation of madness is simply as behaviour out of one's ordinary character, such as when the tricksters instruct Malvolio to perform in ways peculiar for him, including dressing in fashionable, frivolous attire (2.5.141–2). The letter tells him to 'inure thyself to what thou art like to be' (2.5.122–3), and when he does so, observers think he is mad.

Inversion, reversal and opposites

Key quotes

'Be opposite with a kinsman ...' (Malvolio, reading the letter, 2.5.124)

'... I am not what I am.' (Viola, 3.1.126)

'Nothing that is so is so.' (Feste, 4.1.6–7)

'A natural perspective, that is and is not!' (Orsino, 5.1.201)

The possibilities associated with Twelfth Night and misrule often involved reversals, mirroring, opposites and an inversion of the natural order. Many dualities in the play, including those discussed below, connect with ideas of inversion, such as one thing being exchanged for another, tensions between binaries, and the overturning of expectations.

Male/female

Viola as Cesario is the ultimate representation of gender inversions. Other illustrations include the illusion of 'identical' male and female twins, with each presenting a kind of inverse of the other. Ultimately, they swap places in the marriage to Olivia, with the confusions and inversions of the previous few months 'righting' themselves in the union between Olivia and Sebastian (mirrored by Orsino and Viola).

Gender power also undergoes inversion in the play, in the context of the roles and expectations restraining women in Elizabethan England. Consider, for example, the degree of power Olivia holds in her court, as well as the level of power Maria wields in setting the trap for Malvolio.

Viola, of course, also plays a key role in driving the action of the play, though this is complicated by the fact that she largely gains power by disguising herself as male.

Wisdom/madness

Malvolio's reversal from controlling others to being at their physical and emotional mercy is the play's darkest inversion. The tricksters' attempt to drive him mad, or at least make others believe he is, is most explicit in the Sir Topas scene (Act 4, Scene 2), when the alleged curate blatantly contradicts Malvolio's (true) observations about the darkness of the room where he is detained. The scene shows society unsettling Malvolio's characteristic certainty, throwing him into a tortured reality where he has no power or freedom. This reversal in status is mirrored by Feste experiencing an opposite inversion – from fool to 'curate', gaining power where he had little.

Restraint/excess

Malvolio's 'puritan' (2.3.119) preoccupation with restraint represents an extreme (with its opposite illustrated in Sir Toby's revelries), and the tricksters take full advantage of this when they slyly instruct him to adopt the most ridiculous reversals in attitude, which he obediently enacts: smiling inappropriately, flirting, wearing preposterous outfits. The cruellest part of this flip is that while he believes he is currying favour with Olivia, whom he aspires to marry, the behaviour is the opposite of what she would find attractive – an inversion of its own.

Outer/inner realities

While the disjunction between Viola's outer and inner realities – her performative and authentic identities – highlights an inversion, there are several representations of stable identities, where outer and inner realities accord. Viola commends the Captain, for example, for his integrity: 'I well believe thou hast a mind that suits / With this thy fair and outward character' (1.2.50–1). It is worth noting that this is a rare occurrence in a play filled with exteriors that hide interiors.

Order/disorder

Malvolio represents order (perhaps in an overly rigid form), while the drunken behaviour of Sir Toby and Sir Andrew represents the wild disorder of Twelfth Night. This juxtaposition is broadly reflected in the journey of the play, which moves from order through disorder and – largely – back to order. However, while the misrule of Twelfth Night is only ever temporary, and thus the play must show things returning to normal, Shakespeare resists neat conclusions, leaving several threads untied. This suggests that the ruptures inversions can create in the social order may not always be fully repaired.

One example is Viola failing to return to her 'woman's weeds' (5.1.257). While the introduction to the New Cambridge edition of the play notes that 'Viola will come to a clear and unambiguous return to gender and social norms in the ... moment of revelation' (p.15), in fact she remains dressed as a boy. This highlights, in all-male casts, the boy actor's gender identity, creating ambiguity in the partnering of Viola and Orsino; Orsino even still calls her 'boy' (5.1.251).

Another example is hinted at in Malvolio's parting threat to be revenged 'on the whole pack of you' (5.1.355), with the actor in some productions gesturing towards the audience, implicating viewers in the cruel pranks played out on the stage.

Time and fate

Key quotes

'Fate, show thy force; ourselves we do not owe.
What is decreed must be; and be this so.' (Olivia, 1.5.265–6)

'O time, thou must untangle this, not I;
It is too hard a knot for me t'untie.' (Viola, 2.2.37–8)

It is difficult to tell from scene to scene how much time is passing in the course of *Twelfth Night*. Before Viola first visits Olivia she is told that Orsino 'hath known you but three days' – and this is only Scene 4 of

Act 1 (I.2–3). Time is passing more quickly in the world of the play than it seems to be, contributing to a dreamlike or fantastical quality.

This quality is emphasised when, in the final scene, Orsino reveals 'three months this youth hath tended upon me' (5.1.88), when it might have seemed only a week or so has passed since Viola and Sebastian landed on the shores of Illyria. What, we might wonder, have Sebastian and Antonio been doing for three whole months? Have Sir Toby and Sir Andrew really been house guests, indulging themselves so extravagantly, for so long?

Although it is difficult to reconcile the play's events with its three-month timeframe, there are many references to the passing of time as a means of resolving conflicts and tensions. Viola realises from the start that she is in a precarious situation, alone in a strange country, declaring 'what else may hap, to time I will commit' (1.2.60). When things become even more difficult – loved by Olivia, in love with Orsino, and deceiving both – she hopes time will 'untangle this' (2.2.37). Reinforcing the bond between the two women, Olivia too feels that time will bring solutions. At first she trusts it to heal her grief, but once she meets Cesario the possibility of love suggests a different path, and she appeals to 'fate' to 'show thy force' (1.5.265). With Sebastian's arrival there is indeed a sense of destiny: when he says to Olivia, 'nature to her bias drew' (5.1.244), he uses a metaphor from the game of bowls – the 'bias' of the ball makes it curve in a certain direction, as if it is inevitable that Olivia is going to meet and marry Sebastian after falling in love with Viola.

Time also brings a form of justice to Sir Toby, who has tormented Sir Andrew and Malvolio for his own idle amusement. In Act 5 he is injured and seeks out a doctor, who – ironically – turns out to be drunk. Feste thinks 'the whirligig of time brings in his revenges' (5.1.353–4), arguing that Malvolio's earlier insults justify the tricksters' treatment of him, and Fabian too insists that 'injuries be justly weighed, / That have on both sides passed' (5.1.346–7). But time's passage has not been kind to Malvolio. While Orsino anticipates a 'golden time' (5.1.359) when the marriages can take place, Malvolio can only look forward to being 'revenged on the whole pack of you' (5.1.355).

DIFFERENT INTERPRETATIONS

Different interpretations arise from different responses to a text. Over time, a text will evoke a wide range of responses from its readers, who may come from various social or cultural groups and live in very different places and historical periods. Responses by critics and reviewers can be published in newspapers, journals and books, both online and in print. They can also be expressed in discussions among readers in the media, classrooms, book groups and so on.

While there is no single correct reading or interpretation of a text, it is important to understand that an interpretation is more than a personal opinion – it is the justification of a point of view on the text. To present an interpretation of a text based on your point of view, you must use a logical argument and support it with relevant evidence from the text.

Critical viewpoints

A performance is itself an interpretation of a play's script, and while you are studying the words, it is important to remember that Shakespeare's plays were written for performance, rather than as literary texts. This means it is valuable to see a production of the play in addition to studying the text. While live productions might not be available to you, there are various film versions and filmed stage versions accessible online. In addition, reviews of live performances can be helpful in showing you how to focus on evidence to support your own interpretations, and they can also offer useful perspectives on the play.

As Penny Gay's introduction to the New Cambridge Shakespeare edition outlines, a selected production history of the play shows how context (historical, social, cultural, political and artistic) dominates interpretive decisions, allowing individual productions to construct different 'versions' of the play. Scanning this section (pp.36–60) will give you some idea of the breadth of interpretations of *Twelfth Night*, and remind you how deeply context influences interpretation: a fact relevant to your own readings of the issues and ideas in this play. As an example of an extreme contextual contrast, we will consider a very early written interpretation of the play by an English critic and a contemporary article by an American academic.

William Hazlitt (1778–1830) wrote *Characters of Shakespeare's Plays* (1817), which shaped much analysis and criticism of Shakespeare's work in the nineteenth century – though over the past two centuries his work has fallen in and out of favour with scholars. Drawing on the characters as an entry point to educate readers on the plays, Hazlitt asserts that *Twelfth Night* is 'full of sweetness and pleasantry' and considers it an innocent, light play:

> ... nonsense has room to flourish ... Nothing is stunted by the churlish, icy hand of indifference or severity. The poet runs riot in a conceit, and idolizes a quibble. His whole object is to turn the meanest or rudest objects to a pleasurable account. The relish which he has of a pun, or of the quaint humour of a low character, does not interfere with the delight with which he describes a beautiful image, or the most refined love. The clown's forced jests do not spoil the sweetness of the character of Viola ... (Hazlitt 1817)

In contrast, in a twenty-first-century discussion, David Carroll Simon examines the darker elements of the play, arguing they are significant because they complicate a reading of *Twelfth Night* as simply a lighthearted comedy. For example, he notes that Malvolio chooses to 'demand better from the world, which entails a seriousness of purpose that is anathema to lightness' (Simon 2019, p.442). He also states (p.448) that the 'affective unpredictability' of the ending is startling, and sees Malvolio's fortunes at the conclusion as further evidence that the play is much more than just a frivolous comedy.

It is also worth exploring reviews of Australian productions of Shakespeare, which illustrates how geographical and social context can influence interpretation. For example, a 2023 Bell Shakespeare production of the play took as one area of focus the issues surrounding gender in *Twelfth Night*, attempting to 'reinstate the dramaturgical effect of an all-male cast without having an all-male cast' (Fairbairn 2023). This dictated casting decisions – such as casting a female actor as 'Malvolia', casting a non-binary actor as Feste, and having the male actor cast as Sebastian also play Viola for most of her scenes. Such an interpretation allowed the production to reflect and explore contemporary preoccupations with the role and expression of gender in society. Some reviews of this production noted that the Bell interpretation 'underscores the play's extant gender ambiguities' (Hirst 2023). The word 'extant' (still existing) reminds us that interpretations, to be valid, must pay attention to the evidence available in the original text. Others felt this production articulated 'the core message which Shakespeare was trying to send – that true love respects no man-made definition or category' (Bailey 2023).

Two interpretations

Reading 1: *Twelfth Night* shows the need for moderation and restraint.

Twelfth Night portrays a world where misrule, excess and disorder lead to confusions, cruelties, mistaken identities, injuries and humiliations. Only when order is restored can there be happy endings (though even then, not for all characters, as misrule sometimes does lasting damage). Although it is not a malicious act, Viola disguising herself as Cesario contributes to most of the confusion in the play, and her swapping of roles can be seen as an example of the traditional Twelfth Night revelries and mayhem that stand in opposition to moderation and restraint. Therefore, this central narrative arc serves as a warning against such misrule.

One of the most explicit cautionary tales against excess and disorder, however, is the subplot featuring Sir Toby: a character warned to 'confine [himself] within the modest limits of order' (1.3.6–7), but who persistently disregards this advice. He is constantly intoxicated – a classic illustration of the very opposite of moderation or restraint – and behaves without consideration for others' feelings. He takes advantage of his niece's hospitality and his friend Sir Andrew's wealth, even irritating Maria – whom he claims to love – with his rowdy, irresponsible behaviour. Worse than simply irresponsible, Sir Toby is cruel to both Sir Andrew and, particularly, Malvolio, on whom he, Maria, Sir Andrew and Feste inflict a disproportionate 'punishment' for Malvolio's insistence on order and propriety. Ultimately, Sir Toby's folly is punished (indicating the play's endorsement of the need for restraint and moderation) when he is attacked by Sebastian (another result of mistaken identity caused by Viola's disguise).

Malvolio – despite trying honourably to maintain order in Olivia's household – perhaps bears some responsibility for his own heartless treatment. He, too, fails to recognise the value in moderation and restraint. His attitudes and behaviour are the opposite of Sir Toby's: he is extreme in his rigid enforcement of puritan order, takes himself far too seriously and has unreasonably ambitious desires (to become a count). These qualities lead Maria and the others to set up their cruel trick punishing him for 'that vice' (2.3.128). Had he shown more balance, he would not have been so disliked, and perhaps not such an easy target. Indeed, his absurd behaviour incited by the fake letter is another example of how a disregard for temperance leads directly to distress and humiliation.

On the other hand, the play applauds Viola's emotional restraint in the form of patience and loyalty. She resists telling Orsino of her love and, ultimately, as she had hoped, time untangles the 'knot' of confusion (2.2.38). In the end she is not only reunited with Sebastian, but also united in love with Orsino.

Reading 2: *Twelfth Night* shows that play and pleasure are necessary parts of life.

Twelfth Night – a play associated with traditional festive revelry – celebrates the joys of playfulness, games, tricks and merriment, and mocks those who do not recognise the value of fun. One central plot deals with the comedy and power of disguise and performance, while the other chronicles a reckless group of pranksters, both endorsing the view that play and pleasure are vital elements of life.

Viola initially disguises herself as a boy to gain employment and protect herself. But it is through this playful experiment with identity that she is able to meet and ultimately find happiness with Orsino, and to facilitate others' happiness, too. For example, Olivia and Sebastian, who might never have met, end up together thanks to Viola's actions. Orsino, who advises Viola to 'be clamorous, and leap all civil bounds' (1.4.20) – in other words, to throw all caution to the wind in desperately seeking Olivia's love – unwittingly bolsters Viola's actions, which then leads to Orsino and Viola falling in love.

In the parallel plot, Sir Toby and Sir Andrew live for the joys of hedonistic pleasure, taking great delight in getting drunk, carefree merrymaking and devising tricks 'for the love of mockery' (2.5.15). Even Maria, who sometimes scolds them for their excesses, happily participates in their trick to punish Malvolio for his sanctimoniousness and his attempts to end their fun. That they are able to punish him so successfully – first by making him humiliate himself, and then by locking him up and undermining his sanity – and that they suffer little retribution for it (on the contrary, Sir Toby and Maria are 'rewarded' with marriage), suggests that *Twelfth Night* values playfulness and indulging in tricks and games over a rigid puritan refusal to celebrate the fun in life.

Twelfth Night shows two realities: one with and one without playfulness, and it is the 'cakes and ale' (2.3.98–9) side of life that is portrayed as being far more enjoyable and desirable.

QUESTIONS & ANSWERS

This section focuses on your own analytical writing on the text, and gives you strategies for producing high-quality responses in your coursework and exam essays.

Essay writing – an overview

An essay on a literary work is a formal and serious piece of writing that presents your point of view on the text, usually in response to a given topic. Your 'point of view' in an essay is your interpretation of the meaning of the text's language, structure, characters, situations and events, supported by detailed analysis of textual evidence.

Analyse – don't summarise

In your essays it is important to avoid simply summarising what happens in a text.

- A **summary** is a description or paraphrase (retelling in different words) of the characters and events. For example: 'Macbeth has a horrifying vision of a dagger dripping with blood before he goes to murder King Duncan.'
- An **analysis** is an explanation of the real meaning or significance that lies 'beneath' the text's words (and images, for a film). For example: 'Macbeth's vision of a bloody dagger shows how deeply uneasy he is about the violent act he is contemplating, and conveys his sense that supernatural forces are impelling him to act.'

A limited amount of summary is sometimes necessary to let your reader know which part of the text you wish to discuss. However, always keep this to a minimum and follow it immediately with your analysis of what this part of the text is really telling us.

Plan your essay

Carefully plan your essay so that you have a clear idea of what you are going to say. The plan ensures that your ideas flow logically, that your argument remains consistent and that you stay on topic. An essay plan should be a list of brief dot points covering no more than half a page.

- Include your central argument or main contention – a concise statement of your overall response to the topic.
- Write three or four dot points for each paragraph, indicating the main idea and evidence/examples from the text. Note that in your essay you will need to *expand* on these points and *analyse* the evidence.

Structure your essay

An essay is a complete, self-contained piece of writing. It has a clear beginning (the introduction), middle (several body paragraphs) and end (the last paragraph or conclusion). It must also have a central argument that runs throughout, linking each paragraph to form a coherent whole. See examples of introductions and conclusions in the 'Analysing a sample topic' and 'Sample answer' sections.

The introduction establishes your overall response to the topic. It includes your main contention and outlines the main evidence you will refer to in the course of the essay. Write your introduction *after* you have done a plan and *before* you write the rest of the essay.

The body paragraphs argue your case – they present evidence from the text and explain how this evidence supports your argument. Each body paragraph needs:

- a strong **topic sentence** (usually the first sentence) that states the main point being made in the paragraph
- **evidence** from the text, including some brief quotations
- **analysis** of the textual evidence, with **explanation** of its significance and how it supports your argument
- **links back to the topic** in one or more statements, usually towards the end of the paragraph.

Connect the body paragraphs so that your discussion flows smoothly. Use some linking words and phrases such as 'similarly' and 'on the other hand', though don't start every paragraph like this. Another strategy is to use a significant word from the last sentence of one paragraph in the first sentence of the next.

Use key terms from the topic – or synonyms for them – throughout, so the relevance of your discussion to the topic is always clear.

The conclusion ties everything together and finishes the essay. It includes strong statements that emphasise your central argument and provide a clear response to the topic.

Avoid simply restating the points made earlier in the essay – this will end on a very flat note and imply that you have run out of ideas and vocabulary. The conclusion should be a logical extension of what you have written, not just a repetition or summary of it. Writing an effective conclusion can be a challenge. Try using these tips:

- Start by linking back to the final sentence of the second-last paragraph, rather than leaping back to your main contention straight away – this helps your writing to flow.
- Use synonyms and expressions with equivalent meanings to vary your vocabulary. This allows you to reinforce your line of argument without being repetitive.
- When planning your essay, think of one or two broad statements or observations about the text's wider meaning. These should be related to the topic and your overall argument. Keep them for the conclusion, since they will give you something 'new' to say but still follow logically from your discussion. The introduction will be focused on the topic, but the conclusion can present a wider view of the text.

Essay topics

1. Although appearances deceive in *Twelfth Night*, reality is revealed in the end.
   Do you agree?
2. The harm caused by the revelry of the minor characters shows the importance of maintaining control and order.
   To what extent do you agree?
3. Both Orsino and Olivia are attracted to Viola, who is never entirely male or entirely female.
   Discuss.
4. The characters find a strong sense of identity through the events of the play.
   Discuss.
5. How does *Twelfth Night* explore the nature of love?
6. The play suggests that gender identity is produced mainly through role-playing and relationships.
   To what extent do you agree?
7. 'I'll be revenged on the whole pack of you!'
   Although *Twelfth Night* is a comedy, its ending is not entirely happy.
   Discuss.
8. 'Dost thou think because thou art virtuous there shall be no more cakes and ale?'
   Twelfth Night suggests that life's pleasures can coexist with its responsibilities.
   Discuss.
9. The line between madness and sanity is often crossed in *Twelfth Night*.
   Do you agree?
10. The plot involving Sir Toby, Sir Andrew and Maria has little to do with the plot involving Viola, Orsino and Olivia.
    Do you agree?

Vocabulary for writing on *Twelfth Night*

Aside: a short speech that the other characters don't hear. Viola's aside at the end of Act 1, Scene 4 – 'Yet a barful strife! / Whoe'er I woo, myself would be his wife' (l.40–1) – lets the audience know she has fallen in love with Orsino.

Blank verse: a form of poetry in which the lines are unrhymed but have a regular metre, usually ten syllables with a rhythmic pattern of alternating weak and strong accents (iambic pentameter). It is the main form of verse used in Shakespearean drama. Orsino's opening line is an example (the bold syllables are the accented, or stressed, syllables):

> If **mu**sic **be** the **food** of **love**, play **on** …

Shakespeare often shows a very close connection between two characters by having one speaker start a line of blank verse and the second speaker finish it.

Comedy: the genre of plays to which *Twelfth Night* belongs. As well as containing comic elements, Shakespearean comedy includes a complication or problem that causes unhappiness, and a resolution in which the problem is solved and one or more couples become engaged or marry.

Dramatic irony: occurs when the reader or audience has access to information the protagonist or other characters do not, allowing them insight into the characters' behaviour or the significance of events. In *Twelfth Night*, dramatic irony results from the audience knowing that 'Cesario' is Viola in disguise.

Soliloquy: a significant speech in which a character explains their true thoughts and feelings to the audience. The character is nearly always alone on stage. Sebastian's soliloquy at the beginning of Act 4, Scene 3 provides a rare insight into his feelings and shows his admiration for Olivia.

Analysing a sample topic

***Twelfth Night* is a play filled with people unable to express their true feelings. Discuss.**

An essay topic that requires you to 'discuss' a prompt statement can feel intimidating because it appears so broad. For example, it does not ask you to decide whether you 'agree' or 'disagree' with the statement – which can help you structure your response. However, the topic will always provide you with tools to start planning your response and filtering the textual evidence you intend to use in your essay. First, identify key terms in the statement – here, *people*, *unable to express* and *true feelings*. These terms will guide you in which aspects of the text to focus on. For example, 'people' indicates you are expected to concentrate on characters (rather than events, setting or technical aspects of the text – although of course these elements are always interlinked and you may wish to discuss some of them in reference to character). The next two key phrases identify themes – the notion of being restrained, hidden or silenced, and the notion of 'true' feelings, which links with both the major theme of love and the idea of disguise and identity.

The next useful step with any topic is to form your central argument or main contention. You should generally be able to express this in a single sentence, and it will articulate your response to the prompt, indicating the direction your essay will take. The brainstorming you did in the first step, along with notes you have previously made when reading your text, should help you decide what position you want to argue. Your contention should be specific and concise, expressing a view on or interpretation of the text – even when the topic does not ask you to 'agree' or 'disagree'.

For the topic above, here are some examples of possible contentions.

- While some characters in *Twelfth Night* are hampered by circumstances and cannot convey their real experiences, others clearly articulate their needs and desires.
- Disguise and constructed identities in *Twelfth Night* are strategies allowing characters to truly express themselves.

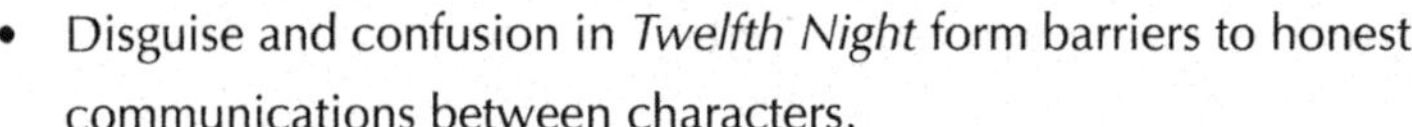

- Disguise and confusion in *Twelfth Night* form barriers to honest communications between characters.

The sample outline below reflects the third contention.

Sample introduction

> Few characters in Shakespeare's *Twelfth Night* are able to openly express their feelings, for a range of reasons. While adopting a disguise can give a character more freedom and opportunities, it can also prevent them from being able to communicate their true feelings and needs, and can even inhibit or misdirect the responses of those around them. When characters are trapped by these barriers, it is only through pure good fortune that happy endings come about. In other cases, convention or circumstance can prevent characters from speaking out, and in these cases, even luck cannot necessarily ensure a happy outcome. At other times still, there are no restrictions to characters actually expressing themselves, but their voices are not properly 'heard', either in the right way or by the right people.

Body paragraph outline

Paragraph 1: Discuss ways in which disguise in the play frees characters or prevents them being able to express themselves truly (include quotes).

- Viola, as Cesario, cannot tell Orsino she loves him: 'As I am man, / My state is desperate for my master's love' (2.2.33–4); 'What I am, and what I would, are as secret as maidenhead' (1.5.177–8); 'She never told her love' (2.4.106). Only the chance appearance of Sebastian releases her from her disguise and allows her to voice her love.
- However, her Cesario disguise *does* allow Viola to make criticisms of male nature that she might not otherwise be at liberty to voice (especially to a duke/count), e.g. that men 'prove ... little in [their] love' (2.4.113–14).

- Feste, disguised as Sir Topas, is able to speak unkindly to Malvolio in a way that his normal role, in which he is subservient to the steward, precludes.

Paragraph 2: Identify characters 'silenced' by circumstance.

- Malvolio yearns for Olivia but their relative social positions prevent him telling her; instead, in Act 2, Scene 5, he fantasises about being married to her (ironically this is overheard by the tricksters, though he does not intend it to be).
- Orsino is drawn to Cesario but, believing him to be a boy, is unable to speak of such a love – only when the disguise is revealed can he say to 'Cesario', 'give me thy hand' (5.1.256).
- We never know Maria's feelings for Sir Toby (whom she marries) – perhaps, for some reason, she is unable to express them.

Paragraph 3: Identify characters who are 'silenced' symbolically, even when they have the means to voice their feelings.

- Malvolio is 'silenced' when locked up – while he can speak to Sir Topas and write a letter, his 'true' suffering is disavowed.
- Sir Andrew is ineffectual in his courting of Olivia; he wishes he had 'followed the arts' (1.3.79) so he might have some hope of eloquently communicating and therefore perhaps reaching her.

Paragraph 4: Acknowledge any evidence conflicting with your view, identifying characters completely free to express themselves honestly.

- Some characters can express their feelings without restriction, but this does not mean they are 'heard' or properly understood. For example, Antonio repeatedly speaks of his 'desire' (3.3.4) for Sebastian, but Sebastian does not acknowledge these feelings.
- Feste, in his role as a fool, has more ability than most to express himself – 'Foolery, sir, does walk about the orb like the sun; it shines everywhere' (3.1.32–3) – but, even when disguised as Sir Topas, his words carry little weight and cannot alter situations.
- These characters are minor rather than central, so they do not undermine the overall contention that the play is heavily peopled by characters unable to express their feelings.

Sample conclusion

While some characters in *Twelfth Night* seem to experience complete freedom to speak their minds, this never guarantees that their needs and desires will be understood or fulfilled. More frequently, characters' social situations prevent them from expressing themselves honestly and, in the case of the protagonist, disguise also hampers open and truthful communication. While the play is a comedy, it also explores darker themes, such as the tragedy of having one's true feelings silenced by external forces.

SAMPLE ANSWER

Although appearances deceive in *Twelfth Night*, reality is revealed in the end.
Do you agree?

Twelfth Night is a play in which, for many characters, little is as it seems: cases of mistaken identity lead to stories of confused love; the festive traditions of disorder and misrule underlie tricks, pranks and reversals; and, despite an ending that indicates the main characters will live happily ever after, some questions remain unanswered and some truths remain unknown. While the disguise and eventual revelation of the identity of the protagonist, Viola, is central to the narrative and traces a journey from deception to reality, even this story is left with hints that all may still not be quite as it appears.

The play's pivotal confusions of identity centre on the shipwrecked twins, Viola and Sebastian, and a third character, Cesario, who is Viola in disguise as a male – a plan she devises to protect herself in Illyria, where she has come ashore. The residents of Illyria are deceived by Cesario's outward appearance, and once Sebastian arrives, his presence adds to the misperceptions, since he and Cesario are indistinguishable: 'An apple cleft in two is not more twin / Than these two creatures'. In the ensuing confusion, Olivia is accidentally betrothed to Sebastian (thinking he is Cesario); Antonio believes he is abandoned by 'Sebastian' ('Will you deny me now?'), though he is speaking to Cesario; and Sir Andrew and Sir Toby are attacked by Sebastian in retribution for their having started a fight with him, believing he is Cesario. However, in the final scene, all these misunderstandings are resolved when the twins are seen together and everyone discovers what has been happening: 'One face, one voice, one habit, and two persons'.

In this same scene, another resolution occurs, unravelling an earlier deception – Fabian reveals the trick played on Malvolio, and Feste confesses his role as Sir Topas: 'I was one, sir, in this interlude'. The public declaration of trickery reveals that Malvolio is not in fact mad, as some have believed, but has been cruelly 'gulled'. Olivia promises that Malvolio 'shalt be both the plaintiff and the judge' of his cause, which suggests that only when deceptions are exposed and facts uncovered can justice be achieved.

However, while the dramatic reveal of the twins' true identities leads immediately to the resolution of all confusions between Sebastian and Cesario, Viola herself remains in partial disguise in the closing moments of the play. While everyone knows who she is, and Orsino has offered her his hand in marriage, Viola remains in her 'masculine usurped attire' rather than returning to her real 'maid's garments'. Peculiarly, Orsino still refers to her – perhaps cheekily, or perhaps subconsciously representing underlying feelings – as 'boy'. While her appearance no longer technically 'deceives', since all around her know she is Viola, her outward form still does not match her inner self, so this is a deception of sorts that is never resolved in the play.

Of course also, we are still witnessing a *performance* (which connects with another of the play's themes: identity, performance and disguise). So at a certain level, 'reality' is never truly reached, even when one layer of disguise and deception is overcome. The audience is still watching actors playing roles. While this is always true of the theatre, it is particularly notable in this play addressing questions of disguise and identity. In *As You Like It* (another Shakespearean play in which the female protagonist dresses as a man), the final moments include the stripping of a last layer of disguise, as the actor playing Rosalind addresses the audience directly, in an epilogue explicitly acknowledging the conventions of the theatre. The fact that Shakespeare chooses, then, not to do this in *Twelfth Night* means that we are intentionally left with illusions: 'A natural perspective, that is and is not'. Outward appearances still deceive and leave us with questions – for example, is 'Viola' truly female (the character) or male (as Cesario's clothing indicates; or since the actor playing her in Shakespeare's time would have been male)?

While the play is a whirl of deceptive appearances hiding inner truths, and while many of these appearances are revealed in the end as disguises and confusions, not everything is fully illuminated by the play's closing moments. Some mysteries and illusions remain, suggesting that layers of disguise and complexity are essential elements of life.

REFERENCES

Text

Shakespeare, W 2017, *Twelfth Night*, ed. E Donno, 3rd edn, The New Cambridge Shakespeare series, Cambridge University Press, Cambridge.

Books

Davis, JM & Frankforter, AD 2004, *The Shakespeare Name Dictionary*, Routledge, New York.

Gurr, A 1992, *The Shakespearean Stage 1574–1642*, 3rd edn, Cambridge University Press, Cambridge.

Hodgdon, B 2002, 'Sexual disguise and the theatre of gender', in A Leggatt (ed.), *The Cambridge Companion to Shakespearean Comedy*, Cambridge University Press, Cambridge, pp.179–97.

Schafer, E 1995, '*Twelfth Night*', in K Parsons & P Mason (eds), *Shakespeare in Performance*, Salamander Books, London, pp.227–32.

Shapiro, M 1995, *Gender in Play on the Shakespearean Stage: Boy Heroines and Female Pages*, University of Michigan Press, Ann Arbor.

Traub, V 2001, 'Gender and sexuality in Shakespeare' in M de Grazia & S Wells (eds), *The Cambridge Companion to Shakespeare*, Cambridge University Press, pp.129–46.

Journal articles

Charles, C 1997, 'Gender trouble in *Twelfth Night*', *Theatre Journal*, vol. 49, no. 2, pp.121–41, https://doi.org/10.1353/tj.1997.0037

Simon, DC 2019, 'Vicious pranks: comedy and cruelty in Rabelais and Shakespeare', *Studies in Philology*, vol. 116, no. 3, pp.423–50, https://doi.org/10.1353/sip.2019.0017.

Websites

Bailey, M 2023, 'Bell Shakespeare puts *Twelfth Night* through the gender blender', *Financial Review*, 27 October, https://www.afr.com/life-and-luxury/arts-and-culture/bell-shakespeare-puts-twelfth-night-through-the-gender-blender-20231027-p5efis

Fairbairn, H 2023, 'Director's notes', https://www.bellshakespeare.com.au/director-notes-twelfth-night-2023

Hazlitt, W 1817, *Characters of Shakespeare's Plays*, https://www.gutenberg.org/cache/epub/5085/pg5085-images.html

Hirst, N 2023, 'Theatre review: *Twelfth Night*, Sydney Opera House', *ArtsHub*, 31 October, https://www.artshub.com.au/news/reviews/theatre-review-twelfth-night-sydney-opera-house-2677070/

Open Source Shakespeare, https://www.opensourceshakespeare.org

Shakespeare's Words, https://www.shakespeareswords.com

Springfels, M 2015, 'Music in Shakespeare's plays', https://www.britannica.com/topic/Music-in-Shakespeares-Plays-1369568/Instrumental-music